The Wonders of the Mass and the Eucharist

Also by Sr. Mary Ann Fatula, O.P.
from Sophia Institute Press:

Heaven's Splendor
Drawing Close to the Holy Spirit

Sr. Mary Ann Fatula, O.P.

The Wonders of the
MASS
and the
EUCHARIST

Insights of the Saints

SOPHIA INSTITUTE PRESS
Manchester, New Hampshire

Sophia Institute Press
Box 5284, Manchester, NH 03108
1-800-888-9344
www.SophiaInstitute.com

Sophia Institute Press is a registered trademark of Sophia Institute.

paperback ISBN 978-1-64413-938-7

ebook ISBN 978-1-64413-939-4

Library of Congress Control Number: 2023937729

First printing

For the glory of the Blessed Trinity

Contents

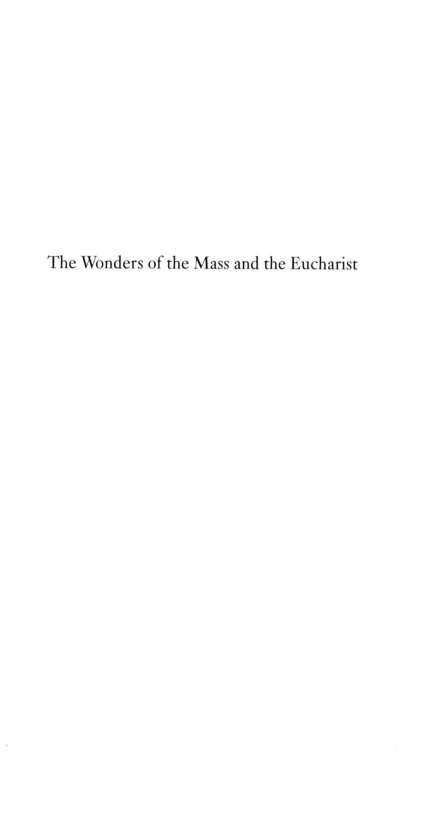

The Wonders of the Mass and the Eucharist

Introduction

Above all other blessings, the most precious gifts of the Trinity to us are the Mass and the Eucharist. Astounding mysteries of love take place at Mass! The Lord Himself makes present to us His Last Supper, death, and glorious Resurrection. And just as He fed His apostles at the Last Supper with *Himself*, in the Eucharist, the sacred fruit of the Mass, the Lord feeds us with His own precious Body and Blood.[1] How different life would be for us if we more deeply understood, loved, and lived these amazing Mysteries of faith!

We desperately *need* the Mass and the Eucharist, far more than we may realize. Countless blessings fill our lives and make our hearts glad, but every day we also face problems, large and small, that threaten to steal our joy. All the while, the Lord is inviting us, "Come to *me* all you that are weary and are carrying heavy burdens, and *I* will give you rest" (Matt. 11:28). The glorious truth is that the Lord Himself, who made this promise to us, is truly present among us at Mass and intimately within us through the Eucharist, giving us *Himself*, lifting our burdens, and filling us with His peace. At a

---

[1] St. John Paul II, Encyclical Letter *Ecclesia de Eucharistia* (April 17, 2003), nos. 11, 12.

deep level, we surely realize this, yet how often we don't allow the Lord to work these miracles of love for us. With our busy lives, it is so easy for us to arrive for Mass at the last minute, to be present in a distracted way, and to leave immediately afterward, with little gratitude for the wonders we have experienced or appreciation for the Lord we bear intimately within us.

How different are the *saints*, who drew their every breath, their very *life*, from the Mass and the Eucharist! This is why St. John Paul II urges us to learn about the wonders of the Mass and the Eucharist from the saints.[2] What a blessing it is to sit at the saints' feet and ponder with them these Sacred Mysteries! In the following chapters, this is what we intend to do. The saints will become our friends and companions, teaching us about the immeasurable blessings the Lord gives us at Mass and through the most precious sacrament of the Eucharist.

The Holy Spirit, who taught the saints, surely will teach us also through them, illumining us and deepening our hunger for the Mass and the Eucharist. In the first chapter, Church Fathers, all Doctors of the Church who were magnificent teachers of the Faith in the early Christian centuries, will enlighten us about the great Mystery of love that takes place at Mass. The first chapter also will clarify the meaning of wonderful words the saints use in their reflections, words such as *Mysteries, sacrament, Divine Liturgy, Mass*, and *Eucharist*.

In the second chapter, the beloved St. John Chrysostom will teach us about the infinite tenderness of the Lord at His Last Supper, death, and Resurrection, the very Mysteries that He makes present to us today in the Mass. In the third chapter, we will learn from the humble and gentle teacher St. Thomas Aquinas about the

---

[2] *Ecclesia de Eucharistia*, 62.

Eucharist, the great Sacrament of Love that refreshes and contents our souls and fills us with the Lord's infinite charity. The amazing St. Catherine of Siena will speak to us with passionate love in the fourth chapter about the power of the Lord's most precious Blood for us. And the wise St. Teresa of Ávila will give us practical advice about receiving the Lord with deeper faith and love.

In the fifth chapter, we will learn about the exquisite grace of longing for the Mass and the Eucharist from two inspiring converts from Anglicanism: St. Elizabeth Ann Seton and St. John Henry Newman. In the sixth chapter, the beautiful St. Thérèse of Lisieux will share with us her prayer and deep desire for daily Mass and Holy Communion. The humble St. John Vianney also will give us wonderful counsels about spending time with the Lord in the Blessed Sacrament. In the seventh and last chapter, the gentle St. Alphonsus Liguori will illumine for us the Lord's desire to be intimately united with us in the Eucharist and will teach us how to grow in our love for Him in the Blessed Sacrament. Finally, the great Pope St. John Paul II will share with us his own tender love for the Lord in the Eucharist and will show us how fulfilled our lives become when we love and live the precious graces of the Mass and the Eucharist.

As we read these chapters, we trust that the Holy Spirit will deepen our love for the Mass and for the Lord in the Eucharist, as well as our closeness with Him and with the Father. And, surely, as our love for the Mass and the Eucharist increases, so, too, will our love and care for one another, especially for those dear to us and those most in need. We will find that our burdens and trials will become lighter because the Lord Himself will be carrying them for us. In a word, our time at Mass and after Holy Communion will begin to make a wonderful difference in our lives.

When we are at Mass and after receiving the Lord in the Eucharist, we may not always have wonderful feelings, which can come and go. But through the insights and inspiration of these beautiful saints, the Holy Spirit surely will fill us with the peace that does not come and go, peace that nothing in the world can give us, or take from us (John 14:27). Sometimes, especially when we are at Mass or after we have received the Lord, tears may fill our eyes—but not because we are sad. The Holy Spirit, who taught the saints, will be tenderly at work within us, opening the eyes of our souls to profound truths, touching our souls with the beauty and wonder of these Sacred Mysteries, in which we are so blessed to participate.

The saints who share with us their beautiful insights in the following pages do so in a way that honors the Mysteries upon which they meditate. A delicious meal deserves to be eaten slowly and truly savored. The saints serve us a feast. Their insights are not meant to be, nor could they ever be, a quick, easy, or superficial read for us. The Mysteries they contemplate are too profound. Oh, but what tremendous blessings will fill us if we are willing to truly *ponder* what the saints say! We will find ourselves returning again and again to their insights, to be inspired and renewed. Their words will stay with us, and their insights will offer us lasting food for our souls.

Let us ask the same Holy Spirit who taught the saints to be our Inner Teacher as well, opening our minds and hearts to amazing wonders we may never have seen or noticed before and deepening our love for the Sacred Mysteries about which the saints so beautifully write. Particular sentences or phrases may stay in our hearts, becoming gentle prayers that we find ourselves repeating during Mass, after receiving the Lord in Holy Communion, and throughout the day. In a special way, let us also ask the Lord to deepen in us the gift of contemplative prayer, the grace to rest in His intimate presence without words or with only a few words, which the Holy Spirit may place in our hearts.

Introduction

May it console us to learn that the saints whom the Holy Spirit so intimately taught, saints who so lovingly share their profound and beautiful insights with us, are our own dear brothers and sisters, weak human beings like us. They, too, were blessed with people they loved, and they, too, struggled with their own trials and heartaches. As their wisdom inspires us, let us also ask them to intercede for us and to obtain for us the grace to do as they did. May we, too, draw from the wondrous Mysteries of the Mass and the Eucharist our own daily strength and love, our own peace and joy and very *life*.

1

Church Fathers
The Mysteries of Faith

The Mass: The Lord's Last Supper, Death, and Resurrection

We owe tremendous gratitude to the Church Fathers who illumine for us in an unparalleled way the wonders that take place at every Mass. Inspired by the Holy Spirit, they teach us that, at Mass, we do not simply remember what the Lord *did* for us at the Last Supper. No, at Mass we are truly *there*! The wonderful St. John Chrysostom, fifth-century bishop of Constantinople, assures us that the altar at every Mass is the very "same" as the Table of the Lord's Last Supper and "has nothing less." At Mass, *we* are in the same "upper chamber" where the apostles were, as the *Lord Himself* celebrates His Last Supper for *us* and gives us His own precious Body and Blood to eat.[3]

As we shall see, it was at the Last Supper that the Lord made present to His apostles His future death and Resurrection. Now, at Mass, we are privileged beyond all telling to be present at these very same saving events. At the beginning of Mass, the bishop or priest urges us to prepare ourselves to celebrate "the *Sacred*

---

[3]   St. John Chrysostom, *Homily 82 on Matthew,* 5.

The Wonders of the Mass and the Eucharist

Mysteries." These "Mysteries" are the Lord's saving deeds of love for us: His Last Supper, death, and Resurrection, completed by His Ascension and Pentecost. At Mass, the Lord allows us to share in all these wondrous, saving events of the past, not by repeating them or recalling them to us but by actually making them present to us today.

Why does the Lord do this for us? We know how we treasure in our hearts and memories the most beautiful events in our lives, the precious times of our past—especially times of joy and celebration and closeness to those dearest to us, times so sweet to us that we never wanted them to end. And now, it isn't enough for us just to remember these most wonderful events of the past. If we could, we would actually *be there, now.* At Mass, this is what the Lord does for us. To fill us with the power and joy and love of His wondrous past saving events for us, He makes them *present* to us *now,* so that they never have to come to an end!

In order to understand more deeply the wonders of the Mass, let us contemplate the mystery of the Last Supper. It was then that the Lord made present to His beloved apostles His future death on the Cross—not in its horror but in its infinite tenderness. On the next day, His apostles would witness His excruciating suffering on the Cross. But they would not know the meaning and ultimate purpose of His death: to give Himself not only for them but also, and most of all, *to* them, in the most intimate and tender way possible, in the sacrament of the Eucharist.

On the Cross, the Lord would give His precious Body to be broken and His sacred Blood to be poured out, but He could not fill His apostles with His own *life* by giving them His precious Body to *eat* and His precious Blood to *drink.* And so, "on the night when He was betrayed," the Lord Jesus took bread, blessed and broke it, and gave it to His apostles, saying, "Take, *eat*; this is my body, which is given for you" (see 1 Cor. 11:23-24; Matt. 26:26; Luke 22:19). "He took a cup ... saying, "*Drink* from it, all of you, for this is my blood" (Matt. 26:27-28). It was in this infinitely tender way that the Lord made His future death present to His beloved apostles.

Through the ministry of His ordained bishops and priests, the Lord now makes present for *us* His past saving death and Resurrection, through making present to us His Last Supper. At Mass, we are not gathered for a beautiful prayer service, simply remembering what the Lord did for us at the Last Supper and on the Cross. We are truly there![4] After offering Himself to His Father on the Cross as a sacrifice of love for our sake, the Lord rose to glorious, risen life, enabling Him to live *within* us even in His physical body. And now, in the Eucharist, the risen Lord Jesus gives Himself to us to eat, to be within us as our strength and our power in every challenge and trial of our lives: "It is no longer I who live, but it is Christ who lives in me" (Gal. 2:20).

The renowned bishop of Rome St. Leo the Great (d. 461), assures us that the Lord so lovingly shared in all our weaknesses except sin, so that He could be the "remedy for us in our misery." The Lord suffered, died, rose to glorious life, was exalted in His Ascension, and sent the Holy Spirit upon us at Pentecost. All these wondrous things the Lord has done for one ultimate purpose: so that He could give His own life not only *for* us but also and most of all *to* us. The Lord heals, in Himself, what is ours,[5] by giving us Himself in the Eucharist, the most precious fruit of the Mass.

If we really believed this, if we really began to "see" with the eyes of faith what is truly taking place at Mass, how tender and glorious the music would be, how filled with worship and praise

[4]   Pope St. John Paul II, *Ecclesia de Eucharistia*, 14.
[5]   St. Leo the Great, *Sermon 67: Sixteenth Sermon on the Lord's Passion*, 5.

and awe we all would be! With the eyes of faith, we would see the Lord Himself, worshipped by myriads of angels as He makes present to us the saving Mysteries of His Last Supper, death, and Resurrection for our sake. We would come to Mass early and enter a church where the congregation is deep in adoration before the Lord, present in their midst. The church would be filled with our brothers and sisters prayerfully awaiting the tremendous event of the Lord's Last Supper and His giving us His precious Body and Blood in the Eucharist to eat and to drink. If we began to see with the eyes of faith these wonders the Lord accomplishes for us at Mass and in the Eucharist, how full of awe and joy and gratitude we would be for the immense privilege of sharing in these tremendous Mysteries!

The Sacred Mysteries

After the sacred moment of Consecration at Mass, the bishop or priest proclaims, "The Mystery of faith!" We respond, "Christ has died, Christ is risen, Christ will come again!" In this way, we proclaim that the "Mystery of faith" that has just taken place in our midst is the Lord's own love-filled death and Resurrection for us.

The Greek word *mysterion* means "what is hidden." The divine "Mysteries" are wondrous, saving events and realities that the Lord Himself accomplishes for us but are hidden from our physical eyes and are seen only with the eyes of faith. These Mysteries are, first and foremost, the saving events of the Lord's Last Supper, death, and Resurrection, whose profound meaning only those with faith can truly "see." The Mysteries are also and inseparably the sacred means by which the Lord makes those saving events present to us today: the Mass and the sacraments, especially the Eucharist. The Lord accomplishes these Mysteries for us through created realities, such as water, bread, and wine, that are perceptible to our senses and through which He fills us with His invisible life-giving grace.

To translate the Greek word *mysterion*, the Western Church began to use the Latin word *sacramentum*, meaning "what is sacred." Eastern Christians, however, have always used the beautiful word *Mysteries* for the sacraments—for example, the Mystery of Baptism, the Mystery of Marriage.

Because the Eucharist is the Lord Himself, the early Christians recognized the Lord's precious Body and Blood as the greatest of the sacraments, or *Mysteries*, through which the Lord imparts to us His invisible life and saving grace. This is why the acclaimed fourth-century bishop St. Cyril of Jerusalem (d. 386) promised his new Christians that he would instruct them in a *special* way about the most treasured of the "Sacred Mysteries," the precious Body and Blood of the Lord in the Eucharist.[6] The word *Eucharist* itself comes from the Greek word *eucharistia*, meaning "thanksgiving," for the gift of the Lord's sacred Body and Blood truly is worthy of our most profound thanksgiving!

Another beautiful word used by the Church Fathers is *liturgy*. Taken from the Greek word *leitourgia*, which means "work on behalf of the people," *Liturgy* refers to the sacred "work" or worship that the Church, united to the Lord, offers to the Father. The Church's liturgy includes the conferring and celebration of the sacraments, the Divine Office, and especially the Mass. Eastern Christians use the beautiful name *Divine Liturgy* for the Mass.

What is the relationship between the Mass and the Eucharist? The Eucharist is not the Mass, but there can be no Eucharist without the Mass, nor Mass without the Eucharist. The Mass is the Eucharistic *Sacrifice* or Eucharistic *Celebration*. It is not a

---

[6] St. Cyril of Jerusalem, *Catechetical Lectures*, 19.1, 11; 22.1, 9.

sacrament but is rather the saving *events* of the Lord's Last Supper, death, and Resurrection for our sake. The sacred fruit of the Mass is the Eucharist, the most precious *Sacrament*. As we have seen, a sacrament is a sacred sign or reality, instituted by the Lord and perceptible to our senses, which actually gives us the invisible grace and reality it signifies.

The glorious bishop of Constantinople St. John Chrysostom (d. 407) explains that the wonders that occur during the Divine Liturgy of the Mass are profound *Mysteries* because the Lord Himself accomplishes them and we see them only with the eyes of faith: "What takes place here requires faith and the eyes of the soul!" Our physical eyes see only what is tangible. This, however, is faith, St. John tells us: "to see the invisible as if it were visible!"[7]

St. Ambrose of Milan (d. 397), the renowned bishop who inspired the conversion of St. Augustine, bishop of Hippo (d. 430), exhorted his own new Christians to use at Mass the sight that is deeper than physical vision. With the eyes of *faith*, they would truly see the wondrous Mysteries taking place in their midst![8] As St. Augustine himself meditated on the mystery of the Eucharist, he cried out to the Father, "Your Son redeemed us with His blood.... I meditate on my Ransom; I *eat* it and *drink* it."[9]

Before the Consecration in the celebration of the Divine Liturgy, Eastern Christians sing the hauntingly beautiful Cherubic Hymn: "Let us who mystically represent the Cherubim, and sing the thrice-holy hymn to the life-creating Trinity, now set aside all earthly cares." After a prayer by the bishop or priest, the entire community continues to sing, "That we may receive the King of

---

[7] St. John Chrysostom, *Second Baptismal Instruction*, 9.
[8] St. Ambrose, *On the Mysteries*, 3.15.
[9] St. Augustine: *Confessions*, 10:43.70.

all, invisibly escorted by angelic hosts."[10] Yes, at Mass the church is filled with the hosts of Heaven, adoring the Lord, who will make His Last Supper present to us and will feed us with His own precious Body and Blood! With the eyes of faith, may we begin to *see* these hosts of Heaven gathered around the Lord Himself as He celebrates His Last Supper for us!

Eastern Christians also pray together this poignant prayer before receiving the Lord in the Eucharist: "O Lord, I believe and profess that You are truly Christ, the Son of the living God.... Accept *me* today as a partaker of *Your Mystical Supper.*" The congregation continues to pray, "O Lord, I also believe and profess that This, which I am about to receive, is truly Your most precious Body and Your life-giving Blood" for the forgiveness of our sins and life everlasting.[11] What a great difference it would make in our lives if every one of us faithfully prayed in this way at every Mass!

There is another tremendous blessing that we can too easily take for granted. The Church tenderly enfolds the sacraments celebrated for the most precious events of our lives, not simply in a beautiful ceremony but rather in the glorious wonders of the Mass! How consoling and strengthening it is for us that our joy-filled Baptisms and Confirmations, our sacred First Holy Communions, our glorious episcopal, priestly, and diaconal Ordinations, our tender Marriages, and our heart-rending funerals are all enveloped by and permeated with the Lord's infinitely loving death and Resurrection! When the most precious events of our lives are celebrated in the

---

[10] "Singing the Cherubikon." Metropolitan Cantor Institute, Byzantine Catholic Archeparchy of Pittsburgh, https://mci.archpitt.org/singing/Divine_Liturgy_Cherubikon.html.

[11] *Prayer before Communion*, St. Michael's Byzantine Catholic Church, https://stmichaelsbyzantine.com/our-faith/prayer-before-communion/.

context of the Mass, the Lord Himself is truly present, conferring His sacraments *and* enfolding us in the wondrous Mysteries of His Last Supper, death, and Resurrection. As the culmination of our celebration, He feeds us with His own precious Body and Blood to be our strength and joy in every part of our lives.

The Mystery of the Crucifixion Made Present to Us at Mass

As we grow to realize that, at Mass, we are present at the Lord's saving death as well as at His Last Supper, the Holy Spirit surely will draw us deeply to the Lord's Crucifixion, which itself is a sacred mystery. What human eyes behold when looking at the Lord on the Cross is a tortured man. What faith sees is the Savior of the world. St. Leo the Great tells us that, through the "mystery" of the Lord's death and Resurrection, even His murderers "could have been saved, if they had believed."[12]

"Father, *forgive* them" (Luke 23:34). The famous bishop St. Gregory the Great of Rome (d. 604) trusted that the Lord's forgiveness of His killers *did* win their conversion and that each later *drank* His precious Blood, the "price of his redemption," in the sacrament of the Eucharist.[13] "O wondrous power of the Cross," St. Leo the Great cries out! "Fount of all blessings, source of all graces!" With infinite love for us, the Lord suffered on the Cross immeasurably more than all our pains, so that He could conquer our sin and death and rise to glorious life, giving us in the Eucharist *His* strength for our weakness, His life for our death.[14]

---

[12] St. Leo the Great, *Sermon 54: Third Sermon on the Passion*, 2.

[13] St. Gregory the Great, *Moral Reflections on Job*, chap. 28, Liturgy Archive, Office of Readings for Friday of the Third Week of Lent, Lectionary Central, http://www.lectionarycentral.com/GregoryMoralia/Book13.html.

[14] St. Leo the Great, *Sermon 59: Eighth Sermon on the Lord's Passion*, 7.

"By a wondrous exchange," the Lord took what was ours and gave us what is His: "salvation for our pain, life for our death."[15] Through the Eucharist, the most precious fruit of the Mass, the Lord now imparts *His own life* to us, so that *He* can be the peace and strength within us for our every weakness and trial: "By his bruises we are healed" (Isa. 53:5).[16] Because we are the members of the Lord's own Mystical Body, [17] these are the very blessings that He pours out upon us and within us at Mass and through the precious sacrament of the Eucharist.

The Power of the Eucharist within Us

The eminent bishop St. Hilary of Poitiers (d. 367), assures us of another profound truth: the Sacrament of the Eucharist deepens our intimate union not only with the Lord Jesus but also with the Father and the Holy Spirit. The Lord Himself abides in the Father, and we abide in the Lord: "I am in my Father, and you in me, and I in you" (John 14:20). When we lovingly receive the Lord in the Eucharist, our intimate union with the Father through grace is also deepened.[18] So, too, our intimacy with the Holy Spirit through grace is strengthened, for the Father gives us the Holy Spirit to be with us and *in* us forever (John 15:26; 14:16-17).

Still another wondrous effect of receiving the Lord in the Eucharist is the deepening of our love and union with one another, especially those dearest to us. The wonderful fifth-century bishop St. Augustine of Hippo assures us that through the Eucharist, we all increasingly become, as St. Paul says, "one body" with the Lord

---

[15] St. Leo the Great, *Sermon 54: Third Sermon on the Passion*, 4.

[16] St. Leo the Great, *Sermon 58: Seventh Sermon on the Lord's Passion*, 4.

[17] St. Leo the Great, *Sermon 63: Twelfth Sermon on the Lord's Passion*, 3.

[18] St. Hilary of Poitiers, *On the Trinity*, 8.15.

(1 Cor. 10:16-17). Created food becomes part of us, but when we feed on the Eucharist, we become more and more deeply "what we receive" and are increasingly transformed into the Lord.[19]

For this very reason, the more faithfully and fervently we receive the Lord in the Eucharist, the more deeply the Lord's own love becomes the source of *our* love. We grow in our desire to show care for the other members of the Lord's Body, particularly the weakest among us. In a most tender way, our love for and union with those dear to us is deepened, especially when we are together at Mass and together receive the Lord in the Eucharist. How many of us have experienced this beautiful truth when we attend Mass with those we love! In ways we cannot fully explain or even understand, our love for one another truly *is* deepened by our being together at Mass and together receiving the Lord in the Eucharist.

Finally, the more we draw our life from the Lord in the Eucharist, the more truly death itself has no power over us. With exquisite beauty, the fourth-century deacon, poet, and Doctor of the Church St. Ephrem of Syria (d. 373) contemplates this mystery of the Lord's conquering our death through His death *even now* through the Eucharist. "All unsuspecting," death had "swallowed up" the body of the Lord. But the Lord, who is life (John 14:6), "slew" death itself by His Resurrection. "Where, O death, is your victory? Where, O death, is your sting?" (1 Cor. 15:55). Now, dwelling within us through the Eucharist, the Lord is not only power for us in our weakness but also unending life for us in our death.[20]

---

[19] St. Augustine, Easter Sermon, 227, St. Anselm Institute for Catholic Thought, https://stanselminstitute.org/files/SERMON%20227.pdf.

[20] St. Ephrem, Deacon, *Sermon on Our Lord*, Office of Readings for Friday of the Third Week of Easter.

The Celebration of the Divine Liturgy in the Early Church

What tremendous joy it is to realize that the Lord makes present to us His saving Mysteries and life-giving power in the Mass, whose prayers we can trace back to the earliest Christian centuries! As we have seen, Eastern Christians' beautiful name for the Mass is the Divine Liturgy. The magnificent fourth-century bishop St. Cyril of Jerusalem gave his newly initiated Christians beautiful instructions in preparing them to participate devoutly in the saving Mysteries of the Divine Liturgy. Today, more than fifteen hundred years later, we recognize as our own the very same prayers of the Divine Liturgy that Cyril celebrated in Jerusalem centuries ago.

As an Eastern bishop, Cyril describes the order and rituals of the Eastern celebration of the Mass, which differ somewhat from the Roman-Rite celebration. Nevertheless, we can hear the celebrated bishop Cyril, so known and loved for the beauty and insight of his baptismal instructions, explaining the profound meaning of the Divine Liturgy of the Mass to *us* today.

The first part of the Mass, the Liturgy of the Word, is meant to deepen our faith in and love for the Lord. We express sorrow for our sins and praise of the Lord and then are fed by the reading of the Sacred Scriptures, which prepare us to enter devoutly into the second part of the Mass, the Liturgy of the Eucharist. It is on this second, most sacred, part of the Mass that St. Cyril focuses his attention.

The Liturgy of the Eucharist begins with the Offertory, the offering by the bishop or priest of the gifts of bread and wine to the Father. At the Consecration, these gifts will be transformed into the Lord's precious Body and Blood. At this sacred moment, the Lord Himself, through the bishop or priest, will make present to us the Sacred Mysteries of His Last Supper and His saving death and Resurrection. St. Cyril explains that, to prepare for the wonders that will be accomplished at the Consecration, the celebrant washes his hands to symbolize *our* desire and willingness to have our hearts cleansed of sin as *we* enter into the Sacred Mysteries.[21]

After the priest washes his hands, the deacon bids us to "receive" and to "kiss" one another with a holy kiss. This is a kiss that "blends our *souls* one with another," Cyril explains. It is a kiss expressing our desire to have only love and forgiveness in our hearts as we prepare for the wonders of the Consecration and of our receiving the Lord in the Eucharist. The Lord Himself commanded us to be reconciled with one another before we offer our gift upon the altar (Matt. 5:24). The "holy kiss" we give to one another at Mass, therefore, is a sacred sign that we have banished from us even the remembrance of wrongs committed against us and that "our souls are mingled together." This is why St. Paul asks us to "Greet one another with a holy kiss" (1 Cor. 16:20) and St. Peter urges us to give one another a kiss of charity (1 Pet. 5:14).[22]

Then begins the Anaphora, the central prayer of the Divine Liturgy. To prepare us to enter into the Sacred Mysteries, the bishop or priest bids us to "lift up" our hearts to the Lord! Cyril explains that we are urged to let go of all earthly concerns and cares so that our hearts may truly be in "Heaven" with the Lord during the Divine Liturgy. We know how many times we can be physically present at Mass while our minds and hearts are a million miles away, even at the most sacred moment of the Consecration. Let us, then, respond to the priest's bidding us to "lift up" our hearts to the Lord, not merely with our voices but also with all our hearts: "We *do* lift them up to the Lord!" In this way, Cyril tells us, we unite ourselves to the praise of the countless hosts of

[21] St. Cyril of Jerusalem, *Catechetical Lectures*, 23.2.
[22] Ibid., 23.3.

Heaven, who are invisibly present, worshipping the Lord. With these, we cry out in worship and praise, "Holy, holy, holy, is the LORD of Hosts!" (Isa. 6:3).[23]

Now we enter into the most sacred part of the Mass, the Consecration. Cyril explains that the *Lord Jesus Himself*, through the ministry of His ordained bishops and priests, changes the bread and wine into His most precious Body and Blood. And He does this precisely so that we may *eat and drink Him*: "Take, eat: This is my body" (Matt. 26:26). "Then he took a cup, and after giving thanks he gave it to them, saying, "*Drink* from it, all of you, for this is my blood" (Matt. 26:27–28). The Lord thus gives *Himself* to us in the Eucharist because He desires to live intimately *within* us. We are not present at Mass simply to *witness* the sacred Meal and Sacrifice that the Lord accomplished for us at His Last Supper, death, and Resurrection. On the contrary, the Lord now makes these Sacred Mysteries present to us at Mass so that we may offer ourselves to the Father with Him, and then *eat* Him, and be filled with *His* love and *life*!

At the Consecration, the Lord Himself, through the bishop or priest, not only speaks the words He used at the Last Supper but also calls down the power of the Holy Spirit upon the bread and wine. Through this *epiclesis*, the bishop or priest, united to the entire community present, asks the Holy Spirit to transform the gifts into the precious Body and Blood of the Lord, for everything that the Holy Spirit touches "is sanctified and changed."[24]

Agreeing with Cyril, the eighth-century St. John Damascene later recalled how it was by the power of the Holy Spirit that the Word Himself "became flesh" (John 1:14) in the womb of Our

[23] Ibid., 23.4, 5, 6.
[24] Ibid., 23.7.

The Wonders of the Mass and the Eucharist

Blessed Mother (Luke 1:34–35). Now, at Mass, the Lord transforms bread and wine into His most precious Body and Blood through His words spoken by the bishop or priest and also by the epiclesis, the invoking of the Holy Spirit upon the gifts and upon all the people present. Just as He accomplished the human conception of God the Son in His Mother's womb, the Holy Spirit at Mass also "is present and does those things which surpass reason and thought." The Lord became flesh in "the holy Mother of God through the Spirit." So, too, the bread and wine are supernaturally transformed into the Lord's sacred Body and Blood through "the invocation and presence of the Holy Spirit."[25]

St. Cyril continues his commentary on the Divine Liturgy, explaining that, after the Consecration, prayers for the sick, the suffering, and all those in need, are offered again to the Lord, now physically present on the altar. Prayer is offered also for those who have died, for, as St. Cyril stresses, such prayer is of great benefit to everyone, living *and* deceased, for whom we intercede during the Sacrifice of the Mass.[26] Following these intercessions, the bishop or priest invites the community to pray with him the prayer that the Lord has commanded us to pray, the Our Father (Matt. 6:9–13).

Cyril begins his beautiful explanation of the Lord's own prayer by expressing the awe we should have at the very words, "Our *Father*." "O most surpassing loving-kindness of God!" Cyril cries out. When we were in the very depths of misery because of our sins, the Lord showered upon us His tremendous mercy. This mercy is so wonderful that, through His saving Mysteries, we who are creatures are now privileged to call *His* own beloved Father not our

---

[25] St. John Damascene, *An Exposition of the Orthodox Faith*, 4.13.

[26] St. Cyril of Jerusalem, *Catechetical Lectures*, 23.8, 9.

"Creator" but rather, with utmost tenderness and from within the very heart of the Lord Jesus Himself, "*Our Father.*"[27]

Furthermore, we pray to our Father "in *Heaven.*" The Heaven where our Father dwells, Cyril assures us, is not only the Heaven we hope to enjoy for all eternity but also and especially the Heaven that is within us. Through the precious gift of grace, we *ourselves* have become the Father's intimate dwelling place and "Heaven." When we pray to our Father "in Heaven," we are asking Him for the grace to know more and more deeply the intimacy of His presence *within* us. And when we pray that the Father's name may be "hallowed," we are praying that His Name may be held holy in us and by us, and that we ourselves may be holy and always treasure His most tender and sacred and intimate name, *Father.*[28]

As a community, we then ask our Father to give us our daily "substantial bread." We do not pray here for bread that feeds merely our bodies, Cyril explains, for created bread is not "substantial bread." The true Bread we ask the Father to give us *every* day in the Our Father is the living Bread, who feeds the very "substance" of our soul. This truly is the Bread from Heaven, the Lord Jesus, who gives Himself to us in the precious sacrament of the Eucharist. It is this Bread, Cyril assures us, for which we pray in the Our Father. The Eucharist alone is the living Bread that feeds and satisfies our entire being, body and soul.[29]

Cyril next describes the beautiful words still used in the Eastern Rites of the Church, as the bishop or priest proclaims, "Holy Gifts to holy people." Yes, Cyril comments, "Holy are the Gifts presented," for they have received the "visitation" of the Holy

27 Ibid., 23.11.
28 Ibid., 23.11, 12.
29 Ibid., 23.15.

Spirit. These sacred Gifts are the precious Body and Blood of the Lord in the Eucharist. "Holy, too," Cyril explains, are we who are present at the Divine Liturgy of the Mass, for we are made holy by the Holy Spirit. Through these beautiful words, "Holy Gifts to holy People," the Lord, through the bishop or priest, draws our minds and hearts to love more deeply His precious Body and Blood, the sacred Gifts we are about to receive. The cantor then invites us to the "Communion of the *Holy Mysteries*," singing a sacred hymn or psalm, such as, "Taste and see that the LORD is good" (Ps. 34:8), for the Lord's precious Body and Blood truly are infinitely sweet.[30]

In approaching with faith and love to receive the Lord in Holy Communion, Cyril teaches us, "make your left hand a throne for the right, as for that which is to receive a King." How exquisite is Cyril's admonition! Let us make our hand a *throne* for the King of Kings, for we hold in our hand the Treasure "more precious than gold," the God of Heaven and earth! Let us then say, with heartfelt love and faith, "Amen" and also bow in worship, responding, "Amen," as we partake of the Lord's precious Blood.[31]

Cyril encourages us not to rush out immediately afterward but rather to wait, adoring and loving the Lord and giving thanks to the Father for making us "worthy," unworthy though we are, to share in such "great mysteries." Cyril concludes by urging us never to willingly deprive ourselves by our absence of these "Holy and Spiritual Mysteries,"[32] for we receive the Lord of Lords Himself and are made "one same body and blood with Him." When we depart from the Divine Liturgy of the Mass, we bear within us

[30] Ibid., 23.19, 20.
[31] Ibid., 23.21.
[32] Ibid., 23.22, 23.

the God of Heaven and earth, who makes us "partakers" of His glorious divine nature (2 Pet. 1:4, RSV).[33]

In his own instructions to his new Christians, St. Ambrose of Milan echoes St. Cyril in urging us to take time to adore the Lord within us, thanking Him for the "*heavenly Mysteries*" in which we have been privileged to share.[34] Let our hearts be full of thanksgiving, for we carry within us the Lord, who is our strength and joy![35]

Faithfully receiving into our inmost being the precious Body and Blood of the Lord, we begin to live more deeply by *His* own life within us. St. Augustine of Hippo reminds us that we "*live by Him, by eating Him.*"[36] The more often we receive the Lord with desire to love Him, the more deeply we will live in that blessed charity that the Lord gives us as a precious fruit of His intimate presence. This is why St. Augustine also cries out in praise of the Eucharist, "O sign of unity! O bond of charity!"[37] After we receive the Lord in Holy Communion, let us beg Him to unite us ever more deeply to Himself and to the members of His Body (1 Cor. 10:17), especially those dearest to us and those most in need.

Finally, how blessed we will be if, after being present at Mass and receiving the Lord's precious Body and Blood in the Eucharist, we continue to "dwell" in Him who dwells in us! Even when the Lord's sacramental presence is no longer there, the sweet effects of His most precious Body and Blood remain within us. St. Augustine encourages us to dwell throughout the day in the Lord's "sweet retreat" within us, His "secret dwelling" in our souls.[38] May

---

[33]   Ibid., 22.3.
[34]   St. Ambrose, *On the Mysteries*, 9.56.
[35]   Ibid., 9.58.
[36]   St. Augustine, *On John*, Tractate 26.19.
[37]   Ibid., Tractate 26.13.
[38]   Ibid., Tractate 25.14, 15.

these saving Mysteries in which we share through the Mass and the Eucharist increasingly become, as they were for the saints, the wellspring from which we draw our own strength and joy and very life.[39]

---

[39] Ibid., Tractate 26.18, 19.

2

St. John Chrysostom
Mysteries of Tenderness

Among all the Church Fathers, the renowned Eastern Doctor of
the Church St. John Chrysostom stands out for the depth and
beauty of his insights on the wondrous Mysteries of the Mass and
the Eucharist. As John reflects especially on the Last Supper, he is
touched by the Lord's infinite *tenderness* in making present to His
beloved apostles His future death and Resurrection and in making
these same Mysteries present to us in the Mass.[40]

A native of Antioch, Syria, John Chrysostom was raised by his
widowed mother, who ensured that he received a superb education,
particularly in rhetoric and the practice of the law. After being
converted from worldly pursuits, John was baptized as a young
adult and withdrew to live a deeply ascetical life. Health issues
that plagued him for the rest of his life forced him to return to
Antioch, where his outstanding qualities were recognized and his
bishop chose him for ordination as a deacon and then as a priest.

Deeply loving and generously serving his community at Antioch
for seventeen years as a priest, John gave magnificent sermons

---

[40] St. John Chrysostom, *Homily 82 on Matthew*, 1.

throughout the year on entire books of the Bible as well as on the divine Mysteries of the Mass and the Eucharist. He also spoke on practical issues of daily living, especially the need to live a good moral life and to care for the poor. John's preaching was filled with such fiery love and insight that he came to be called Chrysostom, "golden mouthed." Often, his congregation responded to his sermons with applause, an acclaim rejected by John, who insisted that the Holy Spirit is the One who truly speaks when hearts are changed.[41]

John's fame in preaching prompted the emperor to have him forcibly taken to the capital city of Constantinople, where he was ordained bishop, serving there for almost five years. His fearless preaching about care for the poor and the perils of riches and his labors to reform and convert the clergy and his people were received by the empress as a condemnation of her lavish lifestyle. Twice she had him banished. John died in 407 while being transported to a remote part of the empire during his second exile. Nearly thirty years after his death, his remains were brought back to Constantinople, where he was honored by the emperor whose mother had so despised him.

In his farewell as he had been taken into exile, John expressed his passionate love both for the Lord and for his beloved people: "I am not afraid of death nor do I long to live, except for your good. Where you are, I am, for we are a single body.... Distance separates us, but love unites us, and death itself cannot divide us."[42]

---

[41] St. John Chrysostom, *Homily 30 on the Acts of the Apostles.*
[42] St. John Chrysostom, *Homily before His Exile*, Office of Readings for the feast of St. John Chrysostom, https://www.liturgies.net/saints/johnchrysostom/catholicreadings.htm.

Inspired, loving words such as these have deeply touched other saints, such as Thomas Aquinas and John Henry Newman, who greatly admired Chrysostom's profound insight and tender heart.[43]

"I love him," writes Newman, for his "kindly spirit," his "intimate sympathy and compassionateness for the whole world," for his "rich vigorous thought and affectionate feeling" that made his writings so "rare and special."[44] Filled with an extraordinary "sweetness," his writings bear the "touch of heaven."[45]

It is especially in his preaching about the sacred Mysteries of the Mass and Eucharist that we find the exquisite "touch of heaven" that so marks Chrysostom's insights. Indeed, to John Chrysostom is attributed the deeply mystical and most often celebrated form of the Divine Liturgy in the Eastern Churches. Chrysostom himself loved St. Paul, who spoke like a mother to her children and who loved his communities with "fiery warmth" and extraordinary tenderness.[46] In St. Paul, Chrysostom recognized the tenderness of the Lord Himself, who is satisfied with nothing less than intimately, *physically* dwelling within us through the precious sacrament of the Eucharist. Paul's own love was so great that he not only cherished his people in his heart; he also longed to be with them, *physically*, and see them "face to face" (1 Thess. 2:17).[47] "This is truly *fervent* love!"[48] The same affection that attracted Chrysostom to St. Paul inspired Chrysostom's own tenderness in writing about the Lord's

---

[43] St. John Henry Newman, "St. Chrysostom," in *Historical Sketches* (London: Longmans, Green, 1906), vol. 2, p. 236.

[44] Ibid., 5.1; pp. 285, 286, 289.

[45] Ibid., 2.1; p. 234.

[46] St. John Chrysostom, *Homily 3 on First Thessalonians*, verse 19.

[47] St. John Henry Newman, "St. Chrysostom," 4.3; p. 274.

[48] St. John Chrysostom, *Homily 3 on First Thessalonians*, verse 17.

intimate physical presence with us and within us through the
Mysteries of the Mass and the Eucharist.

We "See" the Mysteries of the Mass Only through Faith

John first contemplates the beautiful truth that the Mass and the
Eucharist are Mysteries, infinitely tender "secrets" of divine love
that are hidden from our eyes but that the Holy Spirit enables us to
see with the eyes of faith.[49] The Holy Spirit unveils these Mysteries,
these secrets, to us because of the Lord's intimate friendship with
us, for only to our dearest friends do we open our hearts: "I have
called you friends because I have made known to you everything
that I have heard from my Father" (John 15:15).[50]

At Mass, with our physical eyes, we see bread and wine and
a human being standing at the altar. With the eyes of faith,
however, we see the Lord Himself celebrating His Last Supper
and giving us His precious Body and Blood to receive within us.
To illustrate what it is like to see the Sacred Mysteries with only
our physical eyes and not also with the eyes of faith, John uses
the example of those who are unable to read and who, in looking at the pages of a book, see only marks on paper. In contrast,
those who are able to read can see the wonderful *meaning* of the
letters. With regard to the divine Mysteries of the Mass and the
Eucharist, those who believe are given by the Holy Spirit a new
and deeper set of "eyes," the gift of faith, to behold the *reality*
and the meaning of the glorious treasures hidden within what
is visible to our human eyes.[51]

---

[49] St. John Chrysostom, *Homily 7 on First Corinthians*, 3; *Homily 40 on First Corinthians*, 2.

[50] St. John Chrysostom, *Homily 7 on First Corinthians*, 2.

[51] Ibid.

The Lord, who underwent His Passion, death, and Resurrection with infinite love for us, wants us not only to *remember* these saving acts but also to have them always *present* to us. And this is what He does for us at Mass! Through infinite love for us, the Lord Jesus continues to pour out upon us the grace of the saving Mysteries of His death and Resurrection by means of the sacred table of the Mass.[52]

Chrysostom's beautiful reflections on the Lord's Crucifixion help us to realize what truly takes place at Mass and to appreciate the tremendous wonders that we can see only with the eyes of faith. Matthew recounts how the people who demanded that the Lord should be crucified gladly accepted their guilt and cried out, "His blood be on us and on our children" (Matt. 27:25). Little did they realize how His love would transform the meaning of their words! From the Cross, the Lord *did* pour out His precious Blood upon them. Allowing Himself to be crucified as a criminal among criminals, Jesus submitted Himself to unbearable pain and derision and torture. He allowed His most sacred Blood to flow out from His every wound so that through His Blood our own wounds could be healed.[53]

Because of His infinite love for us, the Lord willingly submitted every part of His body to be tortured. He permitted His sacred head to be pierced with the crown of thorns, His precious face to be spat upon, His entire body to be whipped and struck by those whom He had created out of sheer love. These horrendous things that the Lord allowed the soldiers and the people to do to Him "go beyond all language," John assures us, for they abused and derided Him in every conceivable way.[54]

---

[52] St. John Chrysostom, *Homily 82 on Matthew*, 2.
[53] Ibid.
[54] St. John Chrysostom, *Homily 87 on Matthew*, 1.

The Wonders of the Mass and the Eucharist

The Lord of the universe suffered all these tortures for every one of us, even the apostles who abandoned Him, even those who crucified Him. Jesus went willingly to His death, bearing His Cross as the instrument of His death but also as the instrument of His victory over our sin and death.[55] When we contemplate how the Lord lovingly endured all these cruel tortures for our sake, John asks us, how can our hearts not melt with love in return?[56] At Mass, then, let us see with the eyes of faith and love what is *truly* taking place in our midst, as the Lord makes present to us the mystery of His saving death for us and bathes us in His precious Blood. Let us pray for deepening faith, faith that is not feelings but the *desire* to believe ever more deeply: "I believe; help my unbelief!" (Mark 9:24).

At Mass, We Are Present at the Last Supper

As he contemplates the Mysteries that the Lord makes present to us at the Divine Liturgy, Chrysostom turns from the horrors of the Lord's Crucifixion to the tenderness of His Last Supper. It was at this paschal meal, His final meal with His apostles, that the Lord made present to them, with supreme tenderness, His future death on the Cross. In this way, He comforted and strengthened them to witness the horrors of His Crucifixion on the next day.[57]

"Having loved his own ... he loved them unto the end" (John 13:1). The Lord saved the greatest sign of His love for the night before He was to die so that He could comfort in the most tender way possible the ones who were "His own."[58] Through infinite love for His apostles, the Lord did for them at the Last Supper what

---

[55] St. John Chrysostom, *Homily 85 on John*, 1.
[56] St. John Chrysostom, *Homily 87 on Matthew*, 1.
[57] St. John Chrysostom, *Homily 82 on Matthew*, 1.
[58] St. John Chrysostom, *Homily 70 on the Gospel of John*, 1.

He could not do for them while dying on the Cross. He gave them His precious Body to eat and His sacred Blood to drink, so that they would never have to be deprived of His physical presence, not only with them but also within them.

On this last night before His death, when the apostles were so filled with sorrow and fear, the Lord also comforted them by tenderly having the disciple "whom He loved" lie close to His heart (John 13:23). With immense sweetness, Chrysostom asks why the Lord allowed "such boldness to *them*." The reason was His love, not only for His "beloved disciple" but also for *all* whom the beloved disciple represents, every one of His apostles and every one of us. By having the "one whom He loved" lie close to His heart, Chrysostom explains, the Lord tenderly "calmed *their* despondency." The Lord knew how deeply anxious and troubled His beloved apostles were, for He was about to leave them for a place where they could not yet come (John 13:33). By having John lie close to Him at the Last Supper, the Lord soothed and comforted *all of them*.[59] When we receive the Lord in the Eucharist, we, too, rest on His heart as surely as the beloved disciple did, and we, too, find peace and rest for our souls (John 14:27; Matt. 11:29).

Chrysostom was deeply touched also by the Lord's tender words comforting His apostles, particularly His calling them His "little children." The Lord knew that we treasure most deeply in our hearts the final loving words spoken by those dear to us when they are near death. This is why the Lord spoke so *sweetly* to His apostles: He wanted to inflame their longing never to be separated from Him.[60] But they could not have imagined how the Lord would

---

[59] St. John Chrysostom, *Homily 72 on the Gospel of John*, 1.

[60] St. John Chrysostom, *Homily 27 on First Corinthians*, 5; *Homily 72 on the Gospel of John*, 4.

fulfill their longing by leaving them His intimate physical presence in the sacrament of the Eucharist!

Chrysostom now turns to contemplate the profound mystery of the Lord's making His Last Supper present to *us* in the Mass. That "first Table" of the Last Supper, he assures us, "had no advantage above that which comes after it," the altar at Mass. At every Mass, the Lord Himself "does all," even as He did at the Last Supper, giving us His precious Body and the Cup of His Blood, "filled with power."[61] It is through faith that we "see" these wonders, the *Lord Himself* making present to us His Last Supper through the ministry of the priest, and the precious Body and Blood of the Lord raised up for our worship at the Elevation. "Our bodily eyes see the priest; our spiritual eyes see the great High Priest."[62] The Lord gave Himself to His beloved apostles at the Last Supper, and "*this*," the *Mass*, "*is* that Supper," Chrysostom assures us.[63]

Matthew recounts how the Lord "broke" the bread that He changed into His precious Body (Matt. 26:26). St. Paul also tells us that the "bread that we *break*" at Mass is "a sharing in the body of Christ" (1 Cor. 10:16). Chrysostom tenderly comments that what the Lord suffered on the Cross, with His Body "broken" for our sake, He makes present to us at Mass, in which He "submits to be broken, that He may fill all." The Lord broke the Bread at the Last Supper just as He does on the altar at Mass, so that we may eat Him, receiving Him deep within our being.[64]

---

61 St. John Chrysostom, *Homily 27 on First Corinthians*, 5; *Ninth Baptismal Instruction*, 2.

62 St. John Chrysostom, *Homily 82 on Matthew*, 5; *Eleventh Baptismal Instruction*, 12.

63 St. John Chrysostom, *Homily 27 on First Corinthians*, 6.

64 St. John Chrysostom, *Homily 24 on First Corinthians*, 4.

The Lord's Precious Body and Blood in the Eucharist

John next invites us to ponder the Lord's immeasurable gift of
Himself to us in the Eucharist. Through this, the most precious
gift He could possibly give us, the Lord shows His profound love
and "unspeakable" affection for us all. At His last paschal meal,
His Last Supper with His beloved apostles, the Lord gave them
as their food *Himself.* Now, He does the very same for us in the
Eucharist. "What can be more *tremendous* than this? What could
be more *tender!*" John cries out. The Lord does for us infinitely
more than even the best of lovers can do for those whom they
deeply cherish. He gives us His own precious Body to *eat* and His
own precious Blood to *drink.*[65]

Surely, we would give anything if today we could *see* the Lord,
who loves us with such infinite passion! We would give anything to
be in His presence, to be close to Him not simply in our thoughts
or through our love but *physically*, as the apostles were. Ah, St. John
Chrysostom cries out, "You *do* see Him, you *touch* Him, you *eat*
Him!" The Lord gave Himself not only to His beloved apostles;
He also gives Himself "to *you*," and "not to see only, but also to
touch and *eat* and *receive* within you."[66]

It was not enough for the Lord of Heaven and earth to become
incarnate and even to be tortured and slaughtered for our sake. His
love for us impelled Him to "commingle" Himself with us in the
Eucharist. How blessed we are to partake of His Sacrifice of love
and His sacred Feast! In consuming the Eucharist, our mouths are
"filled with spiritual fire," and our tongues are "reddened" with the
most precious Blood of the Lord Jesus! Chrysostom begs us never
to lose sight of what an immense *privilege* it is to be a partaker of

---

[65] Ibid., 3.
[66] St. John Chrysostom, *Homily 82 on Matthew*, 4.

the Lord's own mystical Supper. We who are weak, sinful human beings *eat* the Lord, whom angels worship in awe. Through the Eucharist, we even become "one flesh" with the Lord Himself.[67]

Chrysostom tenderly urges us to come to the Lord in the Eucharist more eagerly than babes hungry for their mothers' milk. Since the Lord feeds us with nothing less than Himself, may our one sorrow be not to partake of this life-giving food![68] John reminds us of how those who "love strongly" and passionately want to be united as intimately as possible to the ones they love. As for the Lord, only our becoming one with Him could satisfy *His* desire to be physically united to us. Through the most burning love, the Lord has given us the unimaginable gift not only to see and to touch Him but even to embrace and *eat* Him. In the Eucharist, we become one Body with the Lord, "members of His flesh and of His bones," "blended" into His very flesh. The Lord has "kneaded His body with ours, that we might be *one*."[69]

As we consider these Sacred Mysteries, how can our love for the Mass and our longing for the Lord in the Eucharist not grow stronger? When we attend Mass and receive the Lord in the Eucharist, we receive into our inmost being "the Body of Him Who is *God*," "the Body by which we are, and live, by which the gates of hell were broken down and the sanctuaries of heaven opened!" John urges us to fill our minds and hearts with thoughts such as these: "Because of this Body I am not a prisoner but free!" Death itself could not conquer the Lord's body, even though it was tortured and nailed to the Cross. It is this sacred Body of the Lord that we receive in the Eucharist, the Body now risen and glorious

---

[67] Ibid., 5.

[68] St. John Chrysostom, *Homily 82 on Matthew*, 5.

[69] St. John Chrysostom, *Homily 46 on John*, 3.

but still the very Body with which the Lord won our salvation on the Cross: "*This* is that Body, the blood-stained, the pierced, out of which gushed the saving fountains, the one of Blood, the other of water, for all the world!"[70]

If we would ask the devil why he has no power over us, he would answer that it is because of "the Body that was crucified." If we would ask death itself by what power it was conquered and destroyed, death also would cry out, "*This Body.*" Death tried to destroy the Lord by swallowing Him, but it could not "digest" the crucified Body of the Lord of the universe, who rose gloriously from its "jaws."[71]

It is this, His very own Body, victorious over sin and death, that the Lord gives us "to hold and to *eat!*" In a tender meditation, Chrysostom reflects on how those who love cannot get close enough to the ones they love. Loving parents tenderly cover their children with kisses and tell them that they are sweet enough to eat. Satisfying our thirst to have *within* us one we dearly love, the Lord inflames our love for Him by giving us His own precious Body and Blood not only to hold close, but even to eat.[72]

The Power of the Precious Blood of Jesus

The Holy Spirit drew John Chrysostom especially to the mystery and power of the Lord's precious Blood in the Eucharist. In the Mass, the Lord's "Mystical Supper," He has prepared a *Feast* for us. Even if we receive Him under only the species of Bread, we receive the entire Lord, Soul and Divinity, Body and Blood.

When the destroying angel saw merely lamb's blood smeared on the doors of the Hebrews, he did not dare even to approach

---

[70] St. John Chrysostom, *Homily 24 on First Corinthians*, 7.
[71] Ibid.
[72] Ibid.

these doors (Exod. 12:21–23). All the more, John cries out, will the devil not dare to approach those whose lips have become the "doors of a temple which holds Christ!" When the devil sees us returning from the Lord's sacred Banquet, he flees as if he has seen a lion "breathing forth flames from his mouth." Seeing our tongues "stained" with the Lord's own precious Blood, the devil is filled with terror and immediately departs from us.[73]

In receiving the Lord in the Eucharist, we receive the very same precious Blood that "flowed from His side; of *this* do we partake." Wondrous mystery of love! The Lord not only makes present to us in the Mass the pouring out of His precious Blood for us on the Cross. He also gives us the same precious Blood to *drink*.[74] What the Lord could not do on the Cross, He does for us now in the Mass: we *eat* His sacred Body and *drink* His precious Blood. The Lord's infinite desire to be close to us, to be within us, *physically*, could be satisfied only in this wondrous way!

Chrysostom recalls how, at the Lord's Crucifixion, the soldiers pierced His sacred side with a spear. And yet, by means of their intended insult, "an ineffable mystery" was accomplished for us: "At once blood and water came out" (John 19:34). The Blood that poured out of the Lord's sacred side on the Cross is the same precious Blood that we now drink in the sacrament of the Eucharist. This is why John tenderly urges us to approach and receive the Eucharist "as drinking from the very side" of the Lord.[75]

The precious Blood that flowed from the Lord's side on the Cross foreshadowed the Mysteries of the Divine Liturgy and the Eucharist. To know the tremendous power of this Blood, John tells

---

[73] St. John Chrysostom, *Third Baptismal Instruction*, 15; 12.

[74] St. John Chrysostom, *Homily 24 on First Corinthians*, 3.

[75] St. John Chrysostom, *Homily 85 on John*, 3.

us to gaze at its source. This same precious Blood flowed down the Cross from the side of the Lord of Heaven and earth. A soldier pierced the Lord's side, John cries out, "but *I* am the one who has found the treasure and gotten the wealth!"[76] We, too, who drink of the Lord's sacred Blood in the Eucharist know its saving power. We leave Mass clothed with the "armor of the Spirit," surrounded by hosts of angels, and protected by the Lord Jesus Himself.[77]

How tremendous are these awesome Mysteries! The Lord's precious Blood in the Eucharist is a fountain of *life* for us. If we are "scorched" by the heat of temptation, if we are weighed down with struggles and pain, John urges us to come to the fountain of the Lord's Blood, which gives us the power to conquer every force threatening to destroy us. In the Lord's sacred Blood we find comfort, strength, and healing, freedom from the powers of darkness, and peace in the Lord's own glorious love and light.[78]

The Lord's precious Blood is not only power for us but also the means of the deepest intimacy for us. When the Magi drew near to the infant Jesus, they fell down before Him in love and adoration. Today, we behold the Lord not in a manger but on the altar. And although we see the priest with our eyes, we know through faith that the Holy Spirit Himself is "hovering" over the bread and wine that will be consecrated on the altar. At Mass, we do not behold the Body of the Lord as the Magi did, but we *know* and *experience* the power of His sacred Body and Blood in the most intimate way possible. The Magi *saw* the Lord's body, but we *eat* His Body, and we *drink* His precious Blood.[79]

---

[76] St. John Chrysostom, *Third Baptismal Instruction*, 17; 16.

[77] St. John Chrysostom, *Ninth Baptismal Instruction*, 3; *Homily 46 on the Gospel of John*, 3, 4.

[78] St. John Chrysostom, *Homily 46 on the Gospel of John*, 4.

[79] St. John Chrysostom, *Homily 24 on First Corinthians*, 8.

The Wonders of the Mass and the Eucharist

Reverence for the Mysteries That Lift Us to Heaven

John Chrysostom implores us to come to Mass filled with eagerness and awe, for the Lord will feed us with His own precious Body and Blood, before which the angels of Heaven bow in worship.[80] As we behold the Lord sacrificed upon the altar, and the priest and people "empurpled with that precious Blood," John asks us, how can we think that we are on earth? "Are you not rather lifted up to *Heaven?*" What amazing wonders! What infinite love is held out to us in the Mass! The Lord, who reigns in Heaven with His Father, is among us and *within* us and lifts us up to Heaven itself![81]

At the Consecration, when the priest invokes the Holy Spirit and offers "the most dread Sacrifice" of the Divine Liturgy, myriads of angels offer the Lord their love and adoration. With the eyes of faith, let us *see* these powers of Heaven surrounding the altar, worshipping the Lord, who is present upon it![82] Through the wondrous mystery of the Mass, "earth becomes to you a heaven!" On the altar, we gaze at the King of Kings and Lord of Lords, whom we are permitted to *see* here on *earth*—"not angels, but their very Lord!" Nothing on earth is more precious than this: that the God of Heaven and earth is seen and touched and *eaten* by us poor, lowly creatures![83]

John is filled with joy in contemplating these wonders of the Mass and the Eucharist. "What a marvel! What love!" The Lord Jesus, who reigns in glory with the Father and the Holy Spirit, is held "in the hands of all" and gives *Himself* to us as our divine food and drink. We hold the Lord, we embrace Him, we *eat* Him.

---

[80] St. John Chrysostom, *Homily 82 on Matthew*, 5.
[81] St. John Chrysostom, *On the Priesthood*, 3.4.
[82] St. John Chrysostom, *On the Priesthood*, 6.4.
[83] St. John Chrysostom, *Homily 24 on First Corinthians*, 8.

Let us know, through faith, that, at the celebration of the Sacred Mysteries, the altar is laden with heavenly blessings and graces beyond all imagining.[84]

May we enter into the Mysteries of the Mass with faith and love that prepare us even for the moment of our death. The Lord's Mystical Supper, which is the source of our strength and our very life now, is also the power for our attaining unending life in Heaven: "I am the living bread that came down from heaven. Whoever eats of this bread will live forever" (John 6:51). Having shared in the Lord's Mystical Supper as devoutly and as often as we could throughout our lives, we may trust that when we draw near to death, we will do so with confidence and peace, protected from all evil as by the invisible armor of the Lord Himself.[85]

Since the Eucharist is the precious Body and Blood of the Lord of Heaven and earth, Chrysostom stresses that we must never allow this sacred Sacrament to be desecrated in any way. This happens when a nonbeliever or someone known to be committing serious sin is permitted to receive Him. "There is no small punishment for you, if being conscious of any wickedness in anyone, you allow him to partake of this table." John also stresses that the reverence due to this Blessed Sacrament demands that nonbelievers are not to be given the Eucharist, even if they try to do so out of ignorance or good intentions. "Let no one communicate who is not of the disciples. We are to fear God, not man."[86]

St. Paul himself warns us that those who eat and drink unworthily of the Lord, eat and drink judgment to themselves (1 Cor.

[84] St. John Chrysostom, *On the Priesthood*, 3.4; *Third Baptismal Instruction*, 27.
[85] St. John Chrysostom, *Homily 47 on the Gospel of John*, 1; *Homily 24 on First Corinthians*, 8.
[86] St. John Chrysostom, *Homily 82 on Matthew*, 6.

11:27, 29). Chrysostom stresses that if we approach this sacred Sacrament with an "evil conscience," we do so to receive Him not as the source of our life but rather for our punishment.[87] If, however, we come to the Sacrament with faith, love, and repentance for our sins, we receive the Lord for our salvation. Let us then approach Jesus in the Eucharist not with distracted minds and hearts that are attached to sin but rather with love and gratitude for the countless mercies in which we are blessed to share.[88]

The Lord in the Eucharist Unites Us and Impels Us to Care for One Another

We also "ought to approach the Sacred Mysteries" "*bound together.*" With these beautiful words, Chrysostom reminds us that we come to Mass not as isolated individuals but as members of the one Body of the Lord who are called to show care for one another (1 Cor. 12:25). The Lord Himself commands us to be reconciled with one another even before we come to the Sacrifice of the Altar (Matt. 5:24).[89]

Paul, too, reminds us that we who eat one Bread, though many, are one Body (1 Cor. 10:17). When we receive the Lord in the Eucharist, we feed together on the one same Bread of Life. Chrysostom asks us, "And what do we who eat of this Bread become?" We become not many bodies, but *one* Body, the one same mystical Body of the Lord. Chrysostom reminds us that one loaf of bread is composed of many grains. When we feast on the Lord together, we are united to Him and, therefore, in a most profound way, also to one another. "There is not one Body to nourish you, and another for your neighbor, but the very same for all." This is why St. Paul

---

[87] St. John Chrysostom, *Homily 46 on the Gospel of John,* 3.
[88] St. John Chrysostom, *Homily 24 on First Corinthians,* 3.
[89] St. John Chrysostom, *Eleventh Baptismal Instruction,* 33.

stresses that "we *all* partake of the *one* bread" (1 Cor. 10:17). If we are all nourished by the one same Bread of Life and so become one Body with the Lord, surely we are obliged to show the same love, the Lord's own love, to one another. Let us "become also in *this* respect *one*."[90]

Chrysostom turns our attention to the "holy kiss" (2 Cor. 13:12) that we give to one another at Mass. This is no empty gesture but one full of "mystical meaning." Through Baptism, the Holy Spirit has made us a holy "temple" of the Lord (Eph. 2:21). When we kiss each other at Mass, we are kissing the Lord's temple. Through this sacred kiss, our *souls* are united each to the other, and there is deepened in us and among us the beautiful grace that marked the early Church, that all the believers had "*one* heart and soul" (Acts 4:32).[91]

As we have seen, St. Paul stresses that those who eat the Bread and drink the Cup of the Lord unworthily shall be guilty of the Body and the Blood of the Lord (1 Cor. 11:27). Do we not receive the Lord "unworthily" when we also neglect those in need among us? When we pass by the poor and the hungry and pretend not to see, do we not also refuse help to the Lord Himself, who has told us that whatever we do for the least of His brothers and sisters we do for Him (Matt. 25:40)? We honor the Lord at Mass, John reminds us. Let us not dishonor Him in the poor, refusing to give them even a small portion of the goods with which the Lord has so abundantly blessed us.[92]

Indeed, we who have fed on the precious Body and Blood of the Lord ought to be "more gentle than any, and like the angels."

---

90 St. John Chrysostom, *Homily 24 on First Corinthians*, 4.
91 St. John Chrysostom, *Eleventh Baptismal Instruction*, 34; 32.
92 St. John Chrysostom, *Homily 27 on First Corinthians*, 6.

Let us, then, not become cruel by our lack of care for one another. "You have tasted the Blood of the Lord, and not even then do you acknowledge your brother." When we refuse to share even a little of our own food with those in need, we gravely offend the Lord, who has fed *us* with His own precious Body and Blood. If we see the poor and do not help, we are the ones who are truly poor: poor in generosity, poor in charity, poor in virtue.[93]

At Mass, we celebrate the Divine Mysteries *together*, and, as members of His Body, feed *together* on the same Body and Blood of the Lord (cf. 1 Cor. 12:12–13). Let us, then, *remain* one Body of the Lord when we leave Mass. Chrysostom urges us to *continue* to honor the Lord, whom we have received, by showing our love and care for one another. By helping our brothers and sisters in need, we will not "waste the treasure" we have received when we were present at the Sacred Mysteries. "Let us nourish Christ, let us give Him drink, let us clothe Him. *These* things are worthy of that Table."[94]

Finally, John reminds us to return home from the Sacred Mysteries of the Mass and the Eucharist "like lions breathing fire," with our hearts so filled with the Lord's love that even demons fear to approach us.[95] Because of the wondrous Mysteries in which we have shared, we have within and around us the Lord's own protection, more "powerful than any armor," and the Lord's own presence filling our hearts with His peace and joy.[96]

How powerful and touching are these beautiful insights of John Chrysostom on the Sacred Mysteries of the Mass and the Eucharist!

---

[93] Ibid.
[94] St. John Chrysostom, *Homily 24 on First Corinthians*, 7.
[95] St. John Chrysostom, *Homily 46 on the Gospel of John*, 3.
[96] St. John Chrysostom, *Third Baptismal Instruction*, 12.

We now can understand why not only his own communities but also saints such as Thomas Aquinas and John Henry Newman loved him so dearly. May we, too, pray for deeper faith with which to see the precious wonders that St. John Chrysostom illumines so beautifully for us. May his counsels and intercession help us to live ever more deeply and fully the Sacred Mysteries about which he taught with such heartfelt tenderness and burning love!

3

St. Thomas Aquinas
Sweet Sacrament of Love

St. John Chrysostom was especially dear to the thirteenth-century Dominican St. Thomas Aquinas, revered as the "Universal Doctor" or "Teacher" of the Church because of the tremendous clarity, truth, and depth of his insights. Today, more than eight hundred years after Thomas's death at the age of forty-nine, the Church still cherishes his profound insights and works, especially his Eucharistic writings, prayers, and hymns—exquisite treasures such as "O Salutaris," "Tantum Ergo," "Panis Angelicus," and "Adoro Te Devote." Those blessed to know Thomas realized that his poignant Eucharistic writings were the fruit of his own intense devotion to the Lord in the Eucharist. The tears that often flowed down Thomas's face while he celebrated daily Mass tell of his deep love for the Mass and for the Eucharist, the sweet "Sacrament of love" that feeds us with God.[97]

---

[97] Bernard Gui, *The Life of St. Thomas Aquinas*, chap. 15, in *The Life of Saint Thomas Aquinas: Biographical Documents*, ed. and trans. Kenelm Foster (Baltimore: Helicon Press, 1959), p. 37.

The Wonders of the Mass and the Eucharist

Tommaso d'Aquino (1225-1274) was born into an Italian family of nobility. After being educated by the Benedictine monks of Monte Cassino, he studied at the University at Naples, where he met and fell in love with the Dominicans. His family, who had planned that Thomas would become a powerful Benedictine abbot, did all that they could to prevent Thomas from joining this new mendicant order, founded fewer than ten years before Thomas's birth. But Thomas was drawn by temperament and by the Holy Spirit's grace to St. Dominic de Guzman's Order of Preachers. He longed to be united to the Lord as a Dominican, dedicated to proclaiming to all the world the truth of the Lord Jesus, committed to poverty, contemplation, and sacred study, to liturgical prayer and community life.

Strengthened by the Lord and with the help of devoted Dominican friars who befriended him, Thomas overcame his family's objections and entered the Order of Preachers, spending several years at the Dominican convents in Naples and then in Paris. It was at Paris that his famed Dominican teacher, Albert "the Great" of Cologne, recognized Thomas's extraordinary gifts of mind, heart, and soul. Albert eventually took Thomas with him when Albert was charged with opening a Dominican house of studies at Cologne. After studying at Cologne with Albert and being ordained a priest, and with Albert's urging and recommendation, Thomas studied theology at the University of Paris and twice served there as a master of theology. Albert remained a faithful friend and devoted advocate of Thomas for the rest of his life.

At Paris, the Lord also gave Thomas another beloved Dominican friend, Reginald of Piperno. The Dominican community at Paris would assign a "socius," a companion and secretary, to each of the brothers teaching at the University of Paris. The community assigned friar Reginald of Piperno as Thomas's socius. It was

Reginald who became Thomas's dearest friend, the one to whom he entrusted the secrets of his soul.[98]

In the following years, Thomas taught theology at the Dominican houses of study in Orvieto, Rome, and Naples. Even as he was dedicated to a scholarly life of intense sacred study, writing, preaching, and teaching, he never ceased to live as a poor, simple friar in community with his Dominican brothers. As a Dominican, Thomas was known in his native Naples as a wonderful preacher whose sermons were filled not only with profound insight into the truth but also with a "sweet graciousness" that reflected his "kindliness" of heart and soul. Renowned as a brilliant scholar, teacher, and writer, Thomas always remained, first and foremost, an exceedingly humble soul, a "wonderfully kind-hearted man, gentle in speech and generous in deed."[99]

What especially distinguished Thomas was his ability, given by the Holy Spirit, not only to teach and preach the saving truth but also to give profound *reasons* for the truth he taught. He sought these reasons ultimately not in his long hours of study but in his countless nights of prayer. With tears, he constantly turned to the Holy Spirit, begging from Him the grace to understand more deeply the profound truths he was contemplating and that he would generously share with others.[100] And because his teaching and preaching were completely informed by his prayer, Thomas taught and wrote only what he himself contemplated and truly *lived*.[101]

---

[98] First Canonization Enquiry, 61, in Gui, *The Life of Saint Thomas Aquinas: Biographical Documents*, p. 100.

[99] Gui, *Life*, chap. 33, in *The Life of Saint Thomas Aquinas*, p. 51.

[100] William of Tocco, First Canonization Enquiry, 58, in *The Life of Saint Thomas*, p. 98.

[101] Gui, *Life*, chap. 29, in *The Life of Saint Thomas*, p. 47.

The Wonders of the Mass and the Eucharist

An exceedingly prolific writer throughout his life as a Dominican, Thomas labored feverishly in the final years approaching his death, producing more than thirty-three major scriptural, theological, and philosophical works in less than three years. And then everything changed. While Thomas was celebrating Mass in Naples on December 6, 1273, he suffered what seemed to be a breakdown of some kind. He never wrote, taught, or preached again. When urged to resume his theological writing and teaching, Thomas responded that he *could not*: "Such things have been revealed to me that all I have taught and written seems quite trivial to me now."[102]

Perhaps the fevered work that had filled his days and nights for so many years had finally taken its toll. What is certain is that Thomas's experience on that sixth day of December was related to a profound mystical grace granted to him precisely while he was celebrating the wondrous Mysteries of the Mass he so deeply loved.

Even though he was not well, Thomas wanted to comply with the request of Pope Gregory X to serve as a theologian at the Second Council of Lyons. With his companions, Thomas set out on the journey the very next month after his life-changing experience at Naples during Mass. On the way to the council, however, Thomas became extremely ill and spent his final days at the Benedictine abbey at Fossanova.

As he was dying, Thomas asked to receive the Lord in the Eucharist. In the presence of the Blessed Sacrament, about which he had written with such burning love, Thomas exerted tremendous effort and bowed low in adoration. With tears running down his face, he prayed, "O Price of my Redemption, I receive You."[103]

---

[102] Ibid., chap. 27; p. 46.
[103] Ibid., chap. 39; p. 55.

Thomas died on March 7, 1274, surrounded by Benedictine monks honored to have cared for this humble scholar and ardent lover of the Lord in the Eucharist.

The Mass: The Lord's Last Supper and Crucifixion Made Present

As a Dominican preacher and teacher, Thomas constantly drew his insights from Scripture and the Church Fathers. He especially loved St. John Chrysostom, from whose writings he often quotes. Without repeating here the many passages from Chrysostom that touched Thomas's heart, we can see Chrysostom's influence especially in Thomas's writings about the Last Supper and the final words spoken by those we deeply love. It is then, Thomas reminds us, that "our affection for our friends is most enkindled, and the things which affect us most are most deeply impressed in our souls."[104] When the "hour" of the Lord's Passion had come, "having loved his own who were in the world," the Lord passionately and tenderly "loved them to the end" (John 13:1).

With John Chrysostom, Thomas was deeply moved by the infinitely tender way in which the Lord comforted His beloved apostles at the Last Supper. What "burning love" the Lord showed them! How gently He consoled them by calling them "His own."[105] Even more, with immense love and humility, the Lord stooped down to wash their feet, even the feet of Judas, who He knew would betray Him. In this supremely tender act of love, Thomas sees a mystical foreshadowing of the Lord's pouring out of His precious Blood on the Cross to "wash away our sins."[106]

---

[104] St. Thomas Aquinas, *Summa Theologiae*, III.73.5.
[105] St. Thomas Aquinas, *On John 13*, Lecture 1, 1727, 1735, 1736.
[106] Ibid., Lecture 1, 1738, 1741; Lecture 2, 1748.

The Wonders of the Mass and the Eucharist

Now, in the Mass, the Lord makes present to *us* His wondrous Last Supper and saving death and Resurrection. And in the Eucharist, He fills us with His precious Blood, which flowed from His side on the Cross.[107] For this reason, Thomas calls the Eucharist the "Sacrament of the Lord's passion."[108] When we receive the Eucharist, we receive the entire Lord, who pours out upon us the immense blessings that He gained for us on the Cross.[109]

Thomas turns to the mystery that the Lord ultimately makes present to us in the Mass: His saving death on the Cross.[110] The unspeakable sufferings of the Lord were infinitely more than enough to "expiate for all the sins of the whole world, even of a hundred thousand worlds!" And yet it was not these sufferings in themselves that were the means of our salvation. No, Thomas assures us, the Lord Jesus has saved us through the boundless *love* with which He suffered these tortures for our sake.[111]

And His love becomes *ours* through the sacraments, especially Baptism and, most intimately, the Eucharist, in which we become "one mystic person" with Him. As we draw our very life from Jesus, our Head, His own saving love now belongs to all of us as his members.[112] But His love is true power within us only by our being united to Him and our "cleaving" to Him in faith and love.[113]

---

107 St. Thomas Aquinas, *Summa Theologiae*, III.62.5.

108 St. Thomas Aquinas, *On John* 6, Lecture 6, 963.

109 Ibid., Lecture 7, 970; St. Thomas Aquinas, *On First Corinthians*, 11, no. 671.

110 St. Thomas Aquinas, *Summa Theologiae*, III.46.5.

111 St. Thomas Aquinas, *Commentary on the Apostles' Creed*, art. 4; St. Thomas Aquinas, *Summa Theologiae*, III.48.2.

112 St. Thomas Aquinas, *Summa Theologiae*, III.48.2., ad 1; III.8.5.

113 St. Thomas Aquinas, *On John*, 1, lect. 10; *Summa contra Gentiles*, IV.55.30.

St. Thomas Aquinas

This is what we do most deeply at Mass, when the Lord makes present to us His saving death on the Cross, and especially when we receive Him in the Eucharist.[114]

The Precious Sacrament of the Eucharist

Since at Mass we are truly present at the saving events of the Lord's Last Supper, death, and Resurrection, we surely can receive wondrous blessings without receiving the Lord in the Eucharist. But the Lord Himself makes clear that the ultimate *purpose* of His making these saving Mysteries present to us at Mass is so that we will receive His very Body and Blood into our bodies: "Take and *eat*; this is *my body*.... *Drink* ... for this is my blood" (Matt. 26:26–28). With Chrysostom, Thomas tenderly comments that we ourselves long to be with our own loved ones not merely through our thoughts and memories, but also, and most of all, *physically*. This is why the Lord, who passionately loves us, continues to give us His *physical* presence through the Sacrament of the Eucharist.[115]

It is the Eucharist alone that contains the *Lord Himself* and is, for this very reason, the greatest and most precious of the sacraments. All the other sacraments lead us to the Eucharist, as their very purpose and "consummation" of the spiritual life.[116] Thomas explains that a sacrament is a visible sacred sign, instituted by the Lord, which actually gives us the invisible reality and grace it signifies.[117] As we have seen, the sacrifice of the Mass is not a sacrament but the sacred *action* of the Lord making present to us His Last Supper, death, and Resurrection. Thomas further explains that,

[114] St. Thomas Aquinas, *Summa Theologiae*, III.79.7.
[115] Ibid., III.75.1.
[116] Ibid., III.73.3.
[117] Ibid., III.60.2.

at the Consecration of the Mass, the Lord Himself, through His ordained bishops and priests, and through a divine act we can call *transubstantiation*, completely changes the substance of the bread and wine into His most precious Body and Blood, so that only the species of bread and wine remain.[118]

In the precious Sacrament of the Eucharist, the visible signs are bread and wine. But the invisible *reality* concealed under these signs is the precious Body and Blood of the Lord. The sacrament of the Eucharist is no mere symbol or remembrance of the Lord. The Eucharist is the crucified Lord *Himself* "*in very truth.*"[119] Jesus is truly present in the Eucharist, even if no one receives Him. Thomas explains that all the other sacraments need to be *received* in order to be a sacrament. Baptism, for example, is not the baptismal water but the sacrament conferred when the water of Baptism is poured and the words of Baptism are spoken over the person being baptized. In contrast, the Eucharist itself is a sacrament, containing *the Lord Jesus Himself*, even if no one receives the Eucharist or even believes that the Eucharist *is* the Lord's precious Body and Blood.[120]

It is *not* our faith, then, that makes the Lord physically present with and within us in the Eucharist. No, it is faith that enables us to *know* who is truly present: the Lord Himself. The Eucharist *is* the precious Body and Blood of Jesus, whether we believe this or not. Again, Thomas stresses: after the Consecration of the Mass, only the species of bread and wine remain; what is present *is* the Lord's most precious Body and Blood.[121]

---

[118] Ibid., III.75.4; III.75.5.
[119] Ibid., III.75.1.
[120] Ibid., III.73.1, ad 3.
[121] Ibid., III.75.1; III.75.4.

In his beautiful prayer "Adoro Te Devote," Thomas cries out, "Humbly I adore You, hidden God, *concealed under these forms*." Yes, "sight, touch, and taste *are* deceived." What we see, what we taste and smell and touch, *seem* to be bread and wine, but faith tells us the *truth*: the Eucharist is not bread and wine *and* the Lord but only and totally and completely the Lord Jesus *Himself*. "On the cross Your divinity alone was concealed," Thomas prays. "But *here* Your humanity, too, is *hidden*. Believing and trusting *both*, I seek what the penitent thief sought."[122]

We always receive the Lord Himself in the Eucharist, but our being able to receive His *grace* is dependent, first of all, on our not receiving the Lord unworthily, in a state of unbelief or serious sin. Those who do so blaspheme the Lord and sin even more gravely, for they eat and drink "judgment against themselves" (1 Cor. 11:29).[123] Furthermore, we actually receive the graces of the Lord in the Eucharist to the extent that we receive Him with love and faith.[124] It is consoling to realize, however, that faith is not a matter of feeling, for we can have deep faith even when we don't *feel* that we do. The very *desire* to believe *is* belief, as we pray to the Lord, "I believe; help my unbelief" (Mark 9:24). Our "worthily receiving" the Eucharist means that we *want* to believe and to be united to the Lord ever more deeply and that we *want* to love the Lord and to be freed of anything that holds us back from closeness to Him in the Eucharist.[125]

When we are not able to receive the sacrament of the Eucharist itself, Thomas urges us to receive the Eucharist "spiritually,"

---

[122] See also *Summa Theologiae*, III.73.5.
[123] Ibid., III.79.2, ad 2; III.79.3.
[124] Ibid., III.79.3.
[125] St. Thomas Aquinas, *On John* 6, Lecture 7, 976.

through our desire, for even our desire to receive Him fills us with graces flowing from this sacrament.[126] We can "eat" the Lord's sacred Body and "drink" His most precious Blood in this spiritual way, Thomas tells us, by our love and *longing* for Him in the Eucharist.[127] Our very *wanting* to receive the Lord sacramentally is all the more efficacious in gaining precious graces for us because it unites us to the longing of the entire Church for the Lord Jesus in the Eucharist.[128]

Sacrament of Love

How immense and manifold are the blessings that Jesus in the Eucharist pours out upon us, for He is the Lord who is the very source of all grace (John 1:16)![129] When we receive the Lord with desire to love Him, He increases within us sanctifying grace and the supernatural virtues, forgives our venial sins, and strengthens us against sinning in the future. The Lord also pours out within us His healing power and imparts His own sweetness to our souls. Most of all, the Lord increases within us His divine charity by deepening sanctifying grace within us. Thomas explains that sanctifying grace is the wondrous supernatural habit that elevates our souls, giving us a created sharing in the Trinity's own divine life and "sweetly" inclining us to supernatural good.[130] It is through this beautiful gift of sanctifying grace that the divine Persons of

---

[126] St. Thomas Aquinas, *Summa Theologiae*, Supplement, 6.1. ad 2; III.73.3, ad 2; *Commentary on John* 6, Lecture 7, 969.

[127] St. Thomas Aquinas, *Commentary on John* 6, Lecture 7; *Summa Theologiae*, III.73.3.

[128] St. Thomas Aquinas, *Commentary on John* 6, Lecture 7, 969.

[129] St. Thomas Aquinas, *Summa Theologiae*, III.79.1.

[130] Ibid., I-II.110.2; I-II.110.4.

the Trinity dwell intimately within us as in Their own Heaven and home (John 14:23).[131]

Sanctifying grace is also the created source of the tremendous supernatural virtue of charity, the virtue that Thomas most deeply associates with the Eucharist.[132] St. Augustine had called the Eucharist the "Bond of charity." Thomas himself treasured this beautiful name for the Eucharist, so fitting because, in this sacred sacrament, we receive the Lord of love Himself.[133] For this very reason, the deepest effect of our devoutly receiving the Lord in the Eucharist is the inflaming and "kindling" of divine charity within us.[134] Thomas explains that charity is the wondrous supernatural virtue of *love*, a created participation in the Holy Spirit, whose very name is Love.[135] This greatest of all the virtues (1 Cor. 13:13)[136] elevates, empowers, and inclines our will *easily* and *sweetly* to love the Trinity above all else and to love everyone else for the sake of the Trinity.[137]

We learn by experience that we were made for love and that nothing makes us happier than truly loving and being loved. And nothing gives us more joy than loving those dear to us. All the more is this true of the supernatural virtue of charity, which is intimate *friendship* love with the infinitely loving and lovable divine Persons of the Trinity.[138] We also learn by experience that nothing is more satisfying to us than *mutual* self-giving love for

[131] Ibid., I.43.5.
[132] Ibid., I-II.110.3; III.79.4.
[133] St. Augustine, *On John*, Tract 26.13; Thomas quotes Augustine in *Summa Theologiae*, III.79.1.
[134] St. Thomas Aquinas, *Summa Theologiae*, III.79.4.
[135] Ibid., II-II.24.7.
[136] Ibid., II-II.23.6.
[137] Ibid., II-II.23.2; II-II.23.1, ad 2.
[138] Ibid., II-II.23.1.

each other's true good. And this is what intimate friendship love is. How much joy it gives us to love our intimate friends, so close to us that we reveal the secrets of our hearts only to them (John 15:15). The virtue of charity is intimate friendship love with the Trinity, making it sweet to us to love the Trinity above all else and to love all others for the sake of the Trinity because they belong to the Trinity.[139] Charity, in this way, is the "mother" of all the other virtues, informing them and directing them to its own purpose and goal, which is to *love*.[140]

We can understand now why Thomas assures us of how easy and *delightful* it is for us to practice this beautiful virtue of charity! Because the divine Persons of the Trinity have created us for love, we are naturally inclined to love and to want to be loved. For this very reason, "no virtue has such a strong inclination to its act as *charity* has, nor does any virtue perform its act with such great pleasure."[141] Charity unites us intimately with the Trinity, so that we *love* and *enjoy* the divine Persons above all else and for Their own sake.[142] And since, in the Eucharist, we receive and *enjoy* the Lord's own intimate love and tender familiarity with us, the Eucharist alone is called the "Sacrament of Charity." Indeed, this precious sacrament is the "sign of *supreme charity* and the uplifter of our hope!"[143] The most wondrous effect of our devoutly receiving the Lord in the Eucharist is this deepening of charity within us. And this very charity makes even sweeter the joy and "spiritual refreshment" the Lord imparts to us through this precious sacrament.[144]

---

[139] Ibid., II-II.23.1, ad 2, 3.
[140] Ibid., II-II.23.2; II-II.23.8, ad 3.
[141] Ibid., II-II.23.2.
[142] Ibid., II-II.23.5, ad 2; II-II.23.6.
[143] Ibid., III.73.3, ad 3; III.75.1.
[144] Ibid., III.79.1.

Furthermore, the supernatural virtue of charity is a created sharing in the Trinity's own infinite love, drawing and enabling us also to love one another with the Trinity's own love.[145] Thomas was struck by St. John Damascene's explanation of why the Eucharist is called Holy "Communion." In this sacred sacrament, our "communion" in love is deepened not only with the Lord but also and inseparably with one another.[146] Surely, we experience this truth when we attend Mass with those we love: as the Lord draws us close to Himself, He also draws us closer to one another in His love. In a wonderful way, the Lord in the Eucharist also deepens our "communion" and bond with others whom we may not even know well but who, for example, attend the same Mass as we do.

Love itself binds and *unites* us to those we love, making us more and more "one." This is why intimate *union* is the sweetest and deepest effect of charity and, therefore, of our receiving Holy Communion. Every time we lovingly receive the Lord, we are more deeply united to one another as members of His Mystical Body, the Church. Though many, we who "partake of the one bread and cup" become "one bread ... one body" (1 Cor. 10:17).[147] The Lord in the Eucharist thus unites and fastens us in charity not only to Himself but also more deeply to one another.[148] Thomas was so touched by this truth that he calls the Eucharist the sacrament of the Church's unity because it is the sacrament of the Lord's *love*.[149]

[145] Ibid., II-II.23.1, ad 2.

[146] St. John Damascene, *An Exposition of the Orthodox Faith*, 4.13; St. Thomas Aquinas, *Summa Theologiae*, III.73.4; III.83.4, ad 3.

[147] St. Thomas Aquinas, *Summa Theologiae*, III.79.5; III.80.4.

[148] St. Thomas Aquinas, *On First Corinthians* 11, no. 654.; *Summa Theologiae*, III.83.4, ad 3.

[149] St. Thomas Aquinas, *Summa Theologiae*, III.83.4, ad 3; III.73.3, ad 3.

The Wonders of the Mass and the Eucharist

Through the Eucharist, Our Venial Sins Are Forgiven

Thomas encourages us with the beautiful truth that it also belongs to the very nature of this beautiful Sacrament of Love that our venial sins are forgiven through it. When we devoutly receive the Lord in the Eucharist, He kindles His own charity within us. It is through this very charity that our venial sins — sins that do not destroy the life of sanctifying grace within us — are forgiven. Thomas was especially touched by what he considered to be St. Ambrose of Milan's assurance that the Eucharist is a powerful and tender "remedy" for our daily infirmities and sins.[150]

We always come to the Lord as weak human beings, but Thomas wonderfully comments that the fire of the Lord's love in the Eucharist is infinitely greater than the power of all our venial sins.[151] Thomas does note that, although the Lord always comes to us full of His divine charity, we are able to *receive* this fire of His charity and forgiveness in the measure of our fervor and desire to love Him.[152] When we receive the Lord, then, let us *ask* Him for His forgiveness and healing of our sins, as well as for true repentance and the grace to avoid future sins. Most of all, let us tell the Lord that we love Him and implore Him to deepen our love for Him.[153]

Thomas encourages us to devoutly receive the Lord even if we have committed many venial sins, for no venial sin, past or present, is more powerful than the Lord's infinite love, through which our sins are forgiven. It is true that our venial sins can hinder our experiencing the "spiritual sweetness" of the Lord's presence within us. And although our venial sins do not destroy the life of charity within us,

---

[150] Ibid., III.79.4.
[151] St. Thomas Aquinas, *Summa Theologiae*, III.79.4, ad 3.
[152] Ibid., III.79.5.
[153] Ibid., III.79.3, ad 1.

they do hinder the *fervor* of our charity. Nevertheless, when we receive the Lord with the desire to love Him, our venial sins *are* forgiven, and we are preserved and strengthened against future sins.[154]

Thomas stresses, however, that mortal sin—sin that destroys the life of sanctifying grace in our souls—is not forgiven through the Eucharist. Those in the state of mortal sin would sin still more gravely if they received the Eucharist without first having their mortal sins forgiven through the Sacrament of Penance. Thomas tenderly adds that those who are *unaware* of the seriousness of their sin, and who have no attachment to it, *do* receive forgiveness of their sins through the Eucharist. In this precious sacrament, they receive deeper charity, which itself increases their sorrow and repentance and obtains for them the forgiveness of their sins.[155]

Finally, Thomas reminds us that the Lord who comes to us in the Eucharist is the very same Lord who, with infinite compassion, performed miracles of healing when He walked on this earth. The same Lord comes to us to heal *our* spiritual and physical illnesses by feeding us with His own sacred Flesh and Blood, which are healing and life-giving.[156] At every Mass, we pray, "Lord, I am not worthy to receive You. But only say the word, and my soul will be *healed*." When we receive the Lord, then, trusting in His infinite mercy, let us not hesitate to ask Him to heal us and our loved ones in every way that we need.

The Sweetness of the Lord's Physical Presence

The Holy Spirit filled Thomas with a special tenderness in writing about another profound effect of receiving the Lord in the

---

154 Ibid., III.79.8; III.79.6.
155 Ibid., III.79.3.
156 St. Thomas Aquinas, *On John* 6, Lecture 6, 959; Lecture 4, 914.

Eucharist: tasting His heavenly "sweetness" within our souls. As we have seen, the Eucharist is the *greatest* sacrament and the purpose and culmination of all the other sacraments because it contains the Lord Himself, who gives Himself to us to eat.[157] And what are the wondrous effects in us of *eating* the Lord of Heaven and earth? "Oh, Thomas cries out, "*Taste* and see that the *Lord is sweet!*" (Ps. 33:9, Vulgate).[158]

Surely from his own experience, Thomas tells us that when we receive the Lord with desire to love Him, He refreshes our souls with a deep spiritual delight. How could it be otherwise, for we feed on the God who is sweetness and goodness itself? The Lord in the Eucharist truly does inebriate us with divine *sweetness* that fills and contents our souls.[159] How many of us have experienced this truth after we have received the Eucharist and, without realizing why, have been moved to tears! We know by experience how good it is simply to *be with* someone we dearly love. No words are needed. Regardless of our struggles and problems, the precious gift of just being physically *close* to our loved one is *sweet* to us. We simply rest with a contented heart in our loved one's presence. If this is so, how much sweeter is the *Lord's* intimate, physical presence in our souls! When we receive the Lord with desire to love Him, He consoles and refreshes us with the infinite "sweetness" of His physical closeness.[160]

The beloved disciple, John, who rested on the Lord's heart at the Last Supper (John 13:23, 25), also recounts the Lord's precious words

[157] St. Thomas Aquinas, *Summa Theologiae*, III.73.3.
[158] The Vulgate is St. Jerome's Latin translation of the Bible, which Thomas used. Psalm 33:9 in the Vulgate is Psalm 34:8 in modern translations.
[159] St. Thomas Aquinas, *Summa Theologiae*, III.79.1, ad 2.
[160] Ibid., III.79.1; III.73.1, ad 1.

to His Father: "All that is mine is yours" (John 17:10, ISV). Surely, these are the words the Lord spoke also to John as he rested on His heart, and to Thomas himself as he tasted the Lord's sweetness in the Eucharist. After receiving the Lord, may we, too, take time just to be with Him and taste how sweet it is to rest on His heart. As St. John Chrysostom assures us, the Lord gives Himself to us in the Eucharist so that we may eat Him and tenderly *"embrace"* Him.[161] May we, too, hear the Lord in the Eucharist say to us, "All that is mine is *yours*." With all our heart, let us say to the Lord in return, "And all that is mine is *Yours*." Resting on the Lord's heart as John did, may we experience the peace of soul, the infinitely sweet "spiritual refreshment," the Lord in the Eucharist gives us by deepening His heavenly charity within us.[162] Surely, this is the very heart of the gift of contemplative prayer, which is deepened in us every time we rest in the Lord after receiving Him in Holy Communion.

As he pondered the Lord's sweetness in the Sacrament of Love, Thomas was drawn to the beautiful name for the Eucharist, "Bread from Heaven," taken from Wisdom 16:20 (NABRE): "You nourished your people with food of angels, and furnished them with bread from heaven ... endowed with all delights." After their Exodus from slavery, the Lord had given to the Israelites as their daily food "manna," or "bread from heaven" (Exod. 16:4; Ps. 105:40), prefiguring the precious Sacrament of the Eucharist.

In his exquisite hymn "Panis Angelicus,"[163] Thomas uses this beautiful name "Bread from Heaven," drawn also from Psalm 78:24. The psalmist tells us that the Father gave His people manna,

---

[161] St. John Chrysostom, *Homily 46 on John*, 3.

[162] St. Thomas Aquinas, *Summa Theologiae*, III.79.1.

[163] This hymn is the last two verses of the "Sequence," which Thomas wrote for the Mass on the feast of Corpus Christi.

bread from Heaven to eat. The Lord Himself assures us that He is living Bread who has come down from Heaven and that those who eat of this Bread will live forever (John 6:51). The Lord in the Eucharist is this true "Bread from Heaven" satisfying our souls with every heavenly delight (Wisd. 16:20).

In the precious Sacrament of the Eucharist, our sacred food is the Lord, who is sweetness itself, the One who quiets our hearts and fills us with His own divine peace and contentment.[164] Thomas's reflections on the Eucharist are filled with this contentment, which he himself experienced as he tasted the Lord's sweetness in the Eucharist. This is why he could so beautifully speak of the Eucharist as the sacrament that "*inebriates*" us with "God's own sweetness."[165] We can taste this heavenly sweetness of the Eucharist when we take time just to *be* with the Lord, to rest close to His heart after Holy Communion or during time we spend before the Blessed Sacrament. Thomas tells us that, in the precious Sacrament of the Eucharist, we feast on the very cause of the angels' and saints' joy and are given the most sacred foretaste of Heaven itself. In receiving the Lord, our deepest longings are fulfilled,[166] for He satisfies every hunger of our souls and refreshes us with His own infinite sweetness.[167]

How amazing is the Lord's tender love for us! If we faithfully attend Mass and lovingly receive the Lord in the Eucharist, if we take the time to rest in the Lord's intimate presence, we will grow to *enjoy* the Lord, to truly enjoy the heavenly sweetness of His intimate physical presence. Thomas again reminds us that we cannot help longing to be *physically close* to someone we love. To

---

[164] St. Thomas Aquinas, *Summa Theologiae*, III.79.1; III.79.8, ad 2.
[165] Ibid., III.79.1, ad 2.
[166] St. Thomas Aquinas, *Commentary on John 6*, lecture 4, 915.
[167] St. Thomas Aquinas, *Summa Theologiae*, III.79.8.

satisfy this longing, which the Lord Himself has placed within us, He promises us the infinite sweetness of His own physical closeness to us in Heaven. Ah, but He does not want to wait until we are in Heaven to be so close to us! And so, even now, as we journey to Heaven, the Lord gives the sweetness of His physical closeness to us in the sacrament of the Eucharist.[168]

We must keep in mind, however, that to *experience* the Lord's sweetness in the Eucharist, we need to *spend time with Him* after we receive Him. We know that when we are eating even delicious food, if we rush through the meal and don't take the time to savor it, we can't truly enjoy it. The food nourishes our bodies, but we don't have any enjoyment in eating it. The same is true of our time with those who are dear to us. If we don't truly spend time, "*waste*" time with them, if we greet them and then quickly leave their company, we can't truly enjoy the sweetness of their company. So, too, when we receive the Lord in the Eucharist. He will always feed and nourish us with Himself. But we will never be able to *savor* the sweetness of His company if we don't take time to enjoy Him: "Taste and see that the LORD is good" (Ps. 34:8). Instead of rushing out immediately after Mass, let us take at least a few moments to close our eyes and simply rest close to the Lord's heart. We don't need many words—or any words at all. Again, this is the very heart of contemplative prayer. When we take time just to be with the Lord, letting Him love and comfort us "like a weaned child" in his mother's arms (Ps. 131:2), *then* we will taste the sweetness of His presence.

Thomas's Exquisite Eucharistic Hymns and Prayers

As we have seen, Thomas is the saint who composed the beautiful Eucharistic hymns that the entire Church uses and treasures today,

[168] Ibid., III.75.1.

beloved hymns such as the "O Salutaris Hostia" and "Tantum Ergo," sung at Benediction of the Blessed Sacrament; the "Pange Lingua," sung at the Mass of Holy Thursday; and treasured hymns and prayers such as "Panis Angelicus" and "Adoro Te Devote." In these hymns, composed for the feast of Corpus Christi, Thomas expresses the tender sentiments of his own soul, his praise and joy, his adoration and passionate love for the precious Sacrament of the Eucharist.

Thomas wrote his Eucharistic hymns at the request of Pope Urban IV when, in 1264, the pope extended to the entire Church the feast of Corpus Christi, already honored in local celebrations. Using and rewriting existing hymns for the Mass and the Divine Office of the feast, Thomas also composed new ones. In his prose writings, Thomas followed the academic customs of his time and often expressed profound truths in a restrained way. In contrast, his beautiful Eucharistic hymns are his magnificent poetry, the *unrestrained* outpourings of his soul, filled with poignancy and lyrical beauty inspired by the Holy Spirit.

Thomas's hymn for Matins, "Sacris Solemniis," sung in the early morning of the feast of Corpus Christi, bids us to welcome the day with glad *shouts* of joy: "May our extreme delight be joined to this sacred, solemn feast! Let our public cries of praise ring out with deepest feeling from the depths of our hearts!" "Let everything be new: our hearts, our voices, our deeds!" In this beautiful hymn, Thomas also expresses his love for the Eucharistic Lord with great tenderness. At the Last Supper, "with *His own hands*, the Lord gave His body to the disciples; all of Him was given to all, given to each." "He gave to the weak His Body, to the sorrowing, the Cup of His Blood." Overcome with the magnificence of the Lord's love, Thomas cries out, "O marvelous, extraordinary Wonder! A servant, poor and humble, consumes God his Lord!"

The hymn "Verbum Supernum," sung at Lauds on the feast of Corpus Christi, has as its concluding verses the "O Salutaris," sung at Benediction of the Blessed Sacrament. In this lovely hymn, Thomas inspires our devotion to the Lord, who, "about to be handed over by a disciple to those jealous of him," first completely "handed *Himself*" over to his disciples, to *eat*. "Born for us, He has given Himself to us to be our intimate Companion now." "Feasting with us," the Lord has given Himself to us "as our Food." "Reigning now in Heaven, He gives Himself to us as our wondrous Reward."

In His "Lauda Sion," the Sequence for the Mass of Corpus Christi and sung after the second reading, Thomas urges us to give voice to shouts of unrestrained joy: "On this solemn day on which we recall the institution of this Table, let our praise be full and resounding, let our souls be full of delight!" May we see with the eyes of faith the truth of the Eucharist: "We believe that bread becomes His Flesh, and wine becomes His Blood. What you do not understand, what you do not see, faith makes firm."

The "Lauda Sion" continues to ring out in praise of the Eucharistic Lord whose love for us is immeasurable. That Jesus would desire such intimate closeness to us that He becomes our very *food*: this is a love before whose depths we must shout our praises! "Praise your Savior, praise as much as you can, as much as you dare; the God who is greater than all praise can *never* be praised enough!" May our celebration of "the living Bread, the Bread of Life," be "full and resounding, delightful and beautiful!" In the verse preceding the last verse, Thomas sings, "The Bread of Angels has been made the Food of pilgrims!" In the name of all of us, Thomas then prays, "Good Shepherd, make us see Your good in the Land of the Living. You who feed us *here*, make us *there* the dinner companions, the coinheritors and intimate friends of the company of the saints!"

The Wonders of the Mass and the Eucharist

Thomas's Vespers hymn for the feast of Corpus Christi, "Pange Lingua," is now sung by the Church throughout the world on the evening of Holy Thursday, as the Eucharist is carried in solemn procession to the Altar of Repose. The last two verses are the "Tantum Ergo," sung at Benediction. In this worship-filled hymn, Thomas urges us to sing of the mystery of our Savior's glorious Body and His most precious Blood, poured out for the Redemption of the world. Because our senses alone cannot tell us the truth about the Eucharist, "let *faith* supply for our senses' defects." The Eucharist is not bread and wine but truly is the *Lord* Himself. Before this most sacred Sacrament, let us cry out in jubilant praise and exaltation and bow low in adoration.

In his beautiful prayer "Adoro Te Devote," Thomas expresses the worship that fills his own heart: "I devoutly adore You, hidden God. My whole heart submits itself to You. Contemplating You, it completely fails." On the Cross, the Lord's divinity was hidden, but in the Eucharist, so, too, is His humanity. Our senses are deceived, but *faith* enables us to see the profound truth of the Eucharist. Alluding to the legend of mother pelicans' feeding their starving young with their own blood, Thomas cries out, "O loving Pelican, Jesus Lord, wash my uncleanness in your Blood, for one drop of Your Blood is enough to cleanse the entire world of every guilt." May Thomas's request in his beautiful prayer be ours: "O Memorial of the Lord's death, living and life-giving Bread! Make my soul *live from You* and ever taste Your sweetness."

The Lord in the Eucharist Brings Us to Eternal Life

The more Thomas fed on the Lord in the Eucharist, the more he *did* long to taste the Lord's sweetness in the joy of Heaven. Daily, Thomas feasted on the Lord's precious Body and Blood at Mass. Surely, he was drawn to meditate often on the Lord's promise that

He is the living Bread who has come down from Heaven and that all those who eat of this Bread will live forever (John 6:51). The Eucharist does bring us to the joy of eternal life, for in the Eucharist we feed on the Lord, who is life (John 14:6) — life for our bodies as well as our souls. Thomas assures us that the Eucharistic Lord is the power within us, even now, for our future resurrection, when our bodies will "share in the incorruption and the glory" of our souls, and *unending life* will fill our bodies.[169] The Lord's sacred Flesh in the Eucharist is the very cause within us of the resurrection of our bodies at the end of time.[170]

Thomas recalls how a very special name for the Eucharist is "Viaticum," meaning what goes "with" us on our journey to a destination. In the precious Sacrament of the Eucharist, we receive the Lord, who is our "way" (John 14:6) and who also goes with us to our true home, which is Heaven. By His physical presence within us in the Eucharist, the Lord fills us with *His life* and becomes our power to attain Heavenly glory.[171] Thomas was convinced that we feed on the Eucharistic Lord here on earth ultimately so that we may attain the whole purpose of the Eucharist, the unending joy of Heaven. In the Magnificat Antiphon for the Corpus Christi Vespers, Thomas beautifully expresses how the past, present, and future become one in the Eucharist: "O sacred Banquet, in which we receive Christ; we recall the memory of His passion, our souls are filled with grace, and the pledge of future glory is given to us." How tremendous it is that the Eucharist is not only the foretaste of Heaven here on earth but also the power within us bringing us to Heaven's bliss![172]

---

[169] Ibid., III.79.1, ad 3.

[170] St. Thomas Aquinas, *On John 6*, Lecture 7, 973.

[171] St. Thomas Aquinas, *Summa Theologiae*, III.73.4; III.79.2.

[172] Ibid., III.79.2.

The Wonders of the Mass and the Eucharist

In a most tender way, Thomas himself experienced this truth. As he drew near to his death at the Benedictine Abbey of Fossanova, Thomas asked for the Eucharist to be brought to him. The Benedictine monks caring for him were the privileged witnesses of the intense devotion with which Thomas received the Lord. He had become so weak that he was bedfast. And yet, when the Eucharist was brought to him, with every ounce of his strength, he raised himself from bed and prostrated himself in adoration. With tears streaming down his face, he received the Lord for the last time. Those present could hear him pray, "O Price of my Redemption and Food for my pilgrimage. I receive You. For Your sake I have studied and toiled and kept vigil. I have preached and taught *You*."[173] Surely, at that moment, there must have welled up within Thomas his own prayer in the "Adoro Te Devote": "Jesus, whom I now behold veiled, I ask you to grant that for which I thirst. May I see Your face unveiled, and may the sight of Your glory be my bliss."

To his beautiful prayer, let our hearts cry out, "Amen!" May Thomas, great lover of the Eucharist, obtain for us the grace to receive the Lord of love more fervently, and may the Lord's sweetness in the Eucharist be for us, as it was for Thomas, truly a foretaste of Heaven's bliss.

---

[173] Gui, *Life*, chap. 39, in *The Life of Saint Thomas Aquinas*, p. 55.

4

St. Catherine of Siena and St. Teresa of Ávila
The Power of the Lord's Precious Blood

In this chapter, we will consider the wonderful Eucharistic insights of two marvelous saints who were named the first women Doctors of the Church: St. Catherine of Siena and St. Teresa of Ávila.

St. Catherine of Siena

The fourteenth-century Dominican tertiary St. Catherine of Siena (1347–1380) had a special affection for her Dominican brother, the "glorious" St. Thomas Aquinas, who had contemplated the Truth so deeply and "tenderly."[174] Sharing Thomas's ardent love for the Lord in the Eucharist, Catherine was drawn by the Holy Spirit to focus especially on the precious Blood of Jesus. She knew by faith that, in the "most gracious sacrament" of the Eucharist, we receive the entire Lord, Soul and Divinity, Body and Blood, even when we receive Him under only the species of bread.[175] Catherine's focus on the Precious Blood stemmed from her own experience of the

---

[174] St. Catherine of Siena, *The Dialogue*, 158, trans. Suzanne Noffke, O.P. (New York: Paulist Press, 1980), p. 339.

[175] Ibid., 110; pp. 206, 207.

great power of the Lord's Blood to convert and heal us, to lighten our burdens, and to make every "bitterness" sweet.[176]

Born in Siena, Italy, Catherine was the twenty-third of twenty-four children. She had no formal schooling and, only by a miraculous grace, learned to read and write as an adult. In her youth, she was drawn to a solitary life of prayer, but the Lord called her to serve Him in the world. When she was eighteen, Catherine convinced the "mantellate," a group of widows who wore the Dominican habit, to receive her into their company. Clothed in the Dominican habit, she then dedicated herself to serving the sick and the poor of Siena.

Once, when Catherine was ministering to an abusive woman suffering from a terrible ulcer, she was filled with revulsion. To humble herself, Catherine drank from the putrid water that had been used to wash the woman's sore. Later, the Lord appeared mystically to Catherine and drew her to drink His precious Blood from His side.[177] The Lord also gave Catherine an intense desire to receive Him as frequently as possible and blessed her with a mystical experience in which His precious Blood washed her entire being.[178]

As she continued to care for the sick and the poor of Siena, Catherine attended Mass and received the Lord as often as she could. Even though this was not daily, it was so often that others criticized her for her presumption and boldness.[179] The Dominican

---

[176] St. Catherine of Siena, *Letter* T 264, in *The Letters of St. Catherine of Siena*, vol. 2, trans. Suzanne Noffke, O.P. (Tempe, AZ: Center for Medieval and Renaissance Texts and Studies, 2001), pp. 480, 481.

[177] Bl. Raymond of Capua, *The Life of Catherine of Siena*, 162–163, trans. Conleth Kearns, O.P. (Wilmington, DE: Michael Glazier, 1980), pp. 155–156.

[178] Ibid., 166, 188; pp. 160, 181.

[179] Ibid., 311; p. 288.

Friars were reluctant to give the Eucharist to Catherine because she often fell into ecstasies after receiving the Lord, and they would have to remove her physically from the church.[180]

And yet, Catherine herself assures us, our own hearts would *melt* with love if we truly understood and appreciated the immense privilege that is ours in being able to receive the Lord in the precious Sacrament of the Eucharist. And when we are not able to receive the Lord sacramentally, let us at least "see" and "touch" Him through our faith and desire. Even though we are weak and often lacking in love, we can and *should* always come to the Lord in the Eucharist filled with great desire for Him, for the more we long for Him, the more deeply we receive His blessings.[181]

In 1374, when Catherine was twenty-seven, all of Siena suffered from the ravages of the plague. With tender love, Catherine devoted herself completely to caring for the victims. Her amazing courage and dedication resulted in her being increasingly sought out as an instrument of the Lord's healing and peace. In 1376, the Dominican friar Raymond of Capua, who would be elected master general of the Dominican Order in the very year Catherine died, was appointed her confessor and spiritual director. It was Raymond who became Catherine's dearest friend and advocate. He would make every effort to ensure that she could receive the Eucharist as frequently as she desired, especially when she would come to him like one starving and beg him to give her soul its divine food.[182]

As she continued to minister to the poor and the sick, Catherine was blessed with precious mystical graces related to her deep love for the Mass and the Eucharist. She tells us how, at the

---

[180] Ibid., 188, 407; pp. 181, 371.
[181] St. Catherine of Siena, *The Dialogue*, 111, 110; pp. 209, 210, 207.
[182] Bl. Raymond of Capua, *Life of Catherine*, 314; p. 291.

The Wonders of the Mass and the Eucharist

Consecration of the Mass, she "saw and tasted the depths of the Trinity,"[183] a beautiful grace often given to her. And, after receiving the Lord, she would repeat over and over, "O Trinity eternal, one God."[184] Catherine was also given a deep awareness of the wonderful "imprint" of the Lord's presence and grace, which He leaves in our souls after we receive Him in Holy Communion. She assures us that, even after the Lord is no longer sacramentally within us, the sweet effects of His presence, especially the warmth of His love, remain within us.[185]

Even as she led a deeply mystical life, Catherine gradually became more and more enmeshed in almost every key social and religious issue of her day. People would flock to hear her speak with impassioned love of the Lord and to be strengthened and consoled simply by being in her company. Raymond of Capua tells us that no description could do justice to the "wisdom" of her conversation and "the charm of her manner." Her inspired words, as well as her gracious presence, filled others with such peace and joy that they could only say within themselves, "Lord, it is good for us to be here" (Matt. 17:4).[186] Civil and Church leaders sought Catherine's advice and help. Disregarding the social customs for women of her time, she would travel on missions of peace and would write letters advising and admonishing people of all ranks, civil and ecclesiastical.

Two years before her death, Pope Urban VI called Catherine to Rome to support his papacy and his reform efforts in a divided Church with several papal claimants. With her companions, Catherine

---

[183] St. Catherine of Siena, *The Dialogue*, 111; p. 210.
[184] St. Catherine of Siena, *Prayer* 4, in *The Prayers of Catherine of Siena*, trans. Suzanne Noffke, O.P. (New York: Paulist Press, 1983), p. 42.
[185] St. Catherine of Siena, *The Dialogue*, 112; pp. 211, 212.
[186] Bl. Raymond of Capua, *Life of Catherine*, 27; p. 28.

traveled to Rome, where she continued her fervent prayer and efforts to achieve Church reform and union. During the next two years, her health increasingly deteriorated. At the age of thirty-three, she died in Rome, after receiving the "most consoling sacrament" of the Eucharist.[187] The profound wisdom and love for the Church that overflowed from Catherine and filled her letters and her *Dialogue* gained for her the honor of being named—with St. Teresa of Ávila in 1980—one of the first two women Doctors, or teachers, of the Church.

The Power of the Lord's Precious Blood to Convert Us

What stands out among the Eucharistic graces the Holy Spirit gave to Catherine is her passionate love for the Lord's precious Blood in the Eucharist. Surely this grace stemmed from her longing as a Dominican for the salvation of others, as she united herself to St. Dominic's constant prayer begging for the Lord's mercy upon sinners. Deeply aware of her own weakness, Catherine received the mystical grace of intercession for others in their frailties and sinfulness.

Catherine's compassion for sinners drew her especially to the Lord's precious Blood because she realized that in our blood is our *life* (Lev. 17:11, 14; Deut. 12:23). Our hearts are pierced to the core when we see blood spilling from a loved one who has been hurt. Infinitely more does the precious Blood flowing from the side of Jesus have the power to touch and melt our hearts. The Holy Spirit drew Catherine to the Lord's precious Blood because, in receiving His Blood, we receive the Lord "more quickly and more eagerly," and we are united with Him "more readily and perfectly."[188] Every time we receive the Lord in the Eucharist, we receive His precious

---

[187] Ibid., 364; p. 338.
[188] Ibid., 163; p. 156.

Blood, whose power is enough to conquer the hardness of any heart and whose plenty fills us with love for the Lord and for one another.[189]

This is why Catherine begs us to drink the Lord's precious Blood in the Eucharist and even to "bathe" and to "drown" ourselves in His Blood. In her passionate admonitions to us, Catherine was following in the footsteps of her brother Dominican St. Thomas Aquinas, who, as we have seen, prayed so fervently to the Lord, "Loving Pelican, Jesus Lord, wash my uncleanness with Your Blood, for one drop alone is enough to cleanse the whole world from all its guilt." How much more will we be cleansed, forgiven, and healed by drinking His Blood in the *Eucharist* and by being "bathed" and "washed clean" in His most sacred Blood!

From her youth, Catherine had longed to die as a martyr and to shed her blood for the Lord Jesus, who poured out His own precious Blood for us on the Cross. But the Lord asked her to stay on the earth and to give herself for the salvation of others. She later told her beloved friend and confessor Raymond of Capua that she had paid an immense price for the "surpassing" love and thirst for others' salvation that the Lord had given her, for she had to remain here on earth when her heart longed to be with Him in Heaven.[190]

The Holy Spirit also drew Catherine to pray that even the most hardened sinners would be converted through the power of the Lord's Blood. Once, a Dominican friar begged Catherine to intercede for a man who had led a very sinful life and who was dying a bitter and unrepentant death. Catherine did intercede for him, constantly. With the boldness inspired by intimate love, she

[189] St. Catherine of Siena, *The Dialogue*, 4; p. 32.
[190] Bl. Raymond of Capua, *Life of Catherine*, 216; p. 205.

reminded the Lord that "she *could not allow* the loss" of this man, sinful as he was, whom He had redeemed by His own precious Blood! She pleaded with the Lord that, since He had delayed her coming to Him in Heaven, the only consolation left to her was seeing others converted to Him. In answer to the prayer that He Himself had inspired within her, the Lord did soften the man's heart, inspiring him to seek out the healing grace of Confession, in which he would receive His infinite mercy and forgiveness. The Holy Spirit melted the man's heart, and he was converted completely to the Lord before dying.[191]

In another instance, two notorious criminals in Siena were shouting blasphemies against God as they were being taken to their execution. When Catherine saw them, she began to cry out in prayer, "Oh, tender Lord, these men are your handiwork, redeemed, most tenderly, by your own precious Blood. How can you show such small regard to them?" Catherine recalled to the Lord the thief who had been crucified at His side and to whom He had made this promise: "*Today* you shall be with me in Paradise" (Luke 23:43). "Why did you do this, except to fill with hope *all others?*" She also begged the Lord, "Remember Peter, and Mary the sinful woman, and Matthew the tax collector. You turned your back on none of *them.*" Catherine continued to accompany the cart carrying the two men, tearfully pleading with the Lord to convert them to Himself.[192]

Just as they were approaching the city gate, Catherine mystically saw the "all-merciful" Lord appearing to them, with His precious Blood streaming from His sacred wounds. He urged them to repent, promising them His infinite mercy and forgiveness.

---

[191] Ibid., 225, 226, 227; pp. 213, 214.
[192] Ibid., 228, 229; pp. 216, 217.

Their hearts were pierced. They begged to see a priest, and, with profound sorrow, they made a heartfelt confession of their sins. Then, "with joy in their hearts, they traveled that road to death, more like invited guests on their way to a banquet." As they were being executed, they cried out not in blasphemy but in jubilant praise of their Lord and Savior.[193]

Perhaps the most profound experience of the power of the Lord's precious Blood was given to Catherine when she befriended a young man sentenced to execution. Through her accompanying this young man even to his death, the Lord revealed to Catherine how powerful His precious Blood is to convert us from sin and lift us from despair, to strengthen and comfort and heal us, regardless of how far away from the Lord we have been or how far away we may feel.

Catherine had received word of a young man, Niccolò di Tuldo, who was condemned to beheading in Siena for a political offense. Hearing of his utter despair, Catherine went to comfort and strengthen him in prison. She longed to help free him of bitterness and to ensure that he died a peaceful death by making a good confession and receiving the Lord in the Eucharist. Catherine assured Niccolò of the Lord's tender love for him and the power of His precious Blood to give him a beautiful death. Niccolò was so deeply consoled that he begged her to accompany him to his execution. With Catherine beside him, he told her, he would die full of peace. Overjoyed by his invitation, Catherine ensured that he received the sacrament of Penance. On the morning of his execution, she attended Mass with Niccolò, and he devoutly received the Lord in Holy Communion for the first time in many years. The grace of this Mass and Eucharist filled with ineffable

[193] Ibid., 230; p. 217.

peace the heart of this man who previously had been torn apart by bitterness and despair.[194]

Catherine urged Niccolò to go to his execution inwardly covered with the precious Blood of Jesus, whom he had received in Holy Communion. Her words to him were so tender and comforting that Niccolò begged Catherine to go ahead of him and to wait for him at the place of execution. When he arrived, she continued to speak to him of the power of the precious Blood of Jesus, who loved him so dearly. At his execution, Catherine received his severed head into her hands, as Niccolò's blood flowed onto her clothes.

At the moment of Niccolò's death, Catherine had a mystical vision that so deeply affected her that, immediately afterward, she was impelled to write about it to her beloved friend Raymond of Capua. Catherine recounts how she had accompanied Niccolò, exhorting him to go to his execution as to his "wedding" and assuring him that he would die protected by and bathed in the precious Blood of Jesus. At his execution, Catherine had an intimate vision of the Lord receiving Niccolò's blood into His open side and uniting it with His own sacred Blood. "What tenderness and love," what infinite mercy the Lord showed to Niccolò's soul as he approached the Lord's side, bathed in His precious Blood! As Niccolò entered the Lord's side, he seemed to turn to Catherine, and with love "sweet enough to draw a thousand hearts," he gave her a sign of his undying gratitude. Then the "hands of the Holy Spirit" "locked" him within the paradise of the Lord's heart.[195]

---

[194] St. Catherine of Siena, *Letter* T 273 (DT 31), in *The Letters of St. Catherine of Siena*, vol. 1, trans. Suzanne Noffke, O.P. (Binghamton, NY: Medieval and Renaissance Texts and Studies, 1988), p. 112.

[195] Ibid., p. 110.

The Wonders of the Mass and the Eucharist

Catherine writes to Raymond that, after being assured that Niccolò was now safe, "hidden away" in the Lord's sacred side, her soul "rested in peace and quiet." She was so deeply touched that she did not want to remove Niccolò's blood that had fallen on her clothes. This mystical experience increased Catherine's longing to shed her own blood for the Lord, and it was only with the "greatest envy" of those already in Heaven that she remained on earth.[196]

We can now understand why Catherine begins her letter to Raymond by begging him to be "*engulfed* and *drowned* in the sweet Blood" flowing from the Lord's side. This is the miracle of love that she had witnessed in Niccolò. Through the power of the Lord's precious Blood, this young man who had been so far away from Him, and who was imprisoned in the depths of despair, was drawn intimately close to Him. Wondrous miracle of the Lord's love! Niccolò was blessed to enter into the "secret" of His heart, which overflowed with love for him. From the Lord's sacred side, Niccolò had drunk mystically of His precious Blood, poured out with such "ineffable" love for all the world.[197] This profound experience served to deepen Catherine's trust in the power of the Lord's Blood to soften and convert *any* heart, regardless of how hardened or filled with despair. She would pray constantly that the Lord would "force" the wills of those who are far away from Him and "dispose them to want what they do not want." She begged the Lord to bathe them and the entire world in His mercy, pouring out on them His Blood, shed with such burning love for us on the Cross.[198]

[196] Ibid., pp. 109, 110.
[197] Ibid., pp. 111, 108, 109.
[198] St. Catherine of Siena, *The Dialogue*, 134; p. 276.

The Holy Spirit gave Catherine an especially beautiful insight into the mystery of the Lord's Blood flowing from His side on the Cross. She tells us that the Lord allowed His side to be pierced with a lance so that we could "see" His "inmost heart," His infinite love for us.[199] The Lord chose also to have His precious Blood flow from *every* part of His body, redeeming us not "with just a single drop of his blood ... but with his whole body's pain and blood." It is with the *torrent* of His precious Blood that the Lord has redeemed the entire human race.[200]

Now, especially in the Eucharist, the Lord bathes *us* in the Blood that He shed for us on the Cross. How often Catherine herself experienced the power of this Blood to heal our wounds and turn our hearts to Him![201] She urges us to experience for ourselves how tenderly the Lord in the Eucharist gives us His precious Blood to comfort and strengthen us. By His Blood, He protects and helps us and deepens our trust that absolutely everything that He permits for us is for our true good.[202]

The Lord, who gives us His precious Blood to drink in the Eucharist, also makes His Blood a "bath" to cleanse and heal us from our sins.[203] Even if we have committed the most horrendous of sins, Catherine urges us *never* to despair. The Lord has blessed us with the Sacrament of Penance as a continuing "Baptism," bathing us in the Blood of Jesus to wash away even the most grievous sins we could possibly commit. When our hearts feel sad or cold or closed, when we feel unloved and unlovable and have lost all

<hr/>

[199] Ibid., 126, 75; pp. 245–246, 139.
[200] St. Catherine of Siena, *Prayer* 9; p. 73; *The Dialogue*, 127; p. 246.
[201] St. Catherine of Siena, *Letter* T 101, in *Letters*, vol. 2, pp. 68, 70.
[202] St. Catherine of Siena, *Letter* T 264, in *Letters*, vol. 2, pp. 480, 481.
[203] St. Catherine of Siena, *The Dialogue*, 126; p. 246.

hope, the precious Blood of Jesus has the power to fill us with the light and warmth of *His* love for us. Whatever bitterness and hopelessness we may feel, the Blood of Jesus, shed for us with such burning love, fills us with His peace and lifts us even from the very depths of despair.[204]

Catherine begs us to "run" to this most sacred Blood of the Lord: "Don't let yourself die of thirst when you have it right there before you!" Let us then beg the Lord to immerse and "drown" us in the precious Blood flowing from His sacred side! Our hearts melt when we see blood pouring from a wound suffered by someone we dearly love. Infinitely more, when we truly gaze with faith upon the precious Blood of the Lord Jesus at Mass, our hearts will be drawn irresistibly to Him who loves us so passionately.[205]

The Blood of the crucified Lord is so wonderful, Catherine assures us, that even if we merely call it to mind with faith and love, our burdens will be lightened. In the Lord's Blood, we find peace and joy even in our trials, and we discover the *infinite* love for which we are made. When we are protected by the Lord's precious Blood, everything that the Father permits for us becomes "easy to bear," and absolutely nothing has the power to destroy us.[206]

The Power of the Lord's Precious Blood at Our Death

Catherine's insights on the Lord's precious Blood are especially compelling when she writes about the moment when each of us must face death. "Don't be afraid of dying!" she cries out. Let us place our trust in the mercy of the Lord, whose precious Blood

---

[204] Ibid., 75; p. 138; *Letter* T 210, in *Letters*, vol. 2, p. 236.

[205] St. Catherine of Siena, *Letter* 18 in *Letters*, vol. 1, p. 76; *Letter* T 189 in *Letters*, vol. 2, p. 133.

[206] St. Catherine of Siena, *Letter* T 264, in *Letters*, vol. 2, p. 481.

is our comfort and saving strength.[207] If we keep in mind the burning love with which the Lord shed His Blood for us on the Cross, we will realize that death is not the end of our life but its true beginning. We will grow in our hope and trust that, bathed in His most precious Blood, we will enter through the doors of death into the joy of Heaven.[208]

But let us not be so "foolhardy" as to wait until the moment of our death to turn to the Lord. *Now* is the time to pray for the grace to be converted completely to the Lord. "Reach out trustingly for the blood, no matter *what* sins you have committed,"[209] Catherine begs us. The Lord wants us to trust that His mercy given to us in His precious Blood outweighs the power of absolutely any sin in our life. Indeed, even if *all* the sins that have ever been committed in the world and throughout all of history were gathered together, they would still be an infinitesimal *drop* compared with the infinite *ocean* of the Trinity's love.[210]

Every day, we come face-to-face with our weakness and sin. But the Father wants us *never* to think of our sins without also thinking of the Lord's infinite mercy given to us in His most precious Blood. If we humbly confess our sins and beg for the grace of repentance and conversion, "what remains is mercy," even if we have spent our entire lives in sin. "My mercy," the Father assures Catherine, "is incomparably greater than all the sins" that anyone could ever commit.[211]

"*No one* ought to despair," the Father assures Catherine. The demons are cunning and cruel, especially to those who are dying,

---

[207] St. Catherine of Siena, *Letter* 52, in *Letters*, vol. 1, p. 161.

[208] St. Catherine of Siena, *The Dialogue*, 148; p. 312.

[209] Ibid., 129; p. 260.

[210] St. Catherine of Siena, *Letter* T 314, in *Letters*, vol. 2, p. 486.

[211] St. Catherine of Siena, *The Dialogue*, 66, 132; pp. 124, 268.

attacking them with anxiety, fear, and remorse that plague them even to the point of despair. Catherine urges us to pray for ourselves, for our dying loved ones, and for all the dying, that the protection of the Lord's precious Blood will be upon them and upon us, as we place all our trust in His saving mercy.[212]

To give in to despair by thinking that our sins are greater than the Father's mercy is worse than any other sin we could possibly commit. The Father assured Catherine: "The despair of Judas displeased me more and was a greater insult to my Son than his betrayal had been." This is why Catherine urges us to cry out in prayer, "I will hide myself in his Blood," through which every possible sin is forgiven and healed.[213]

Catherine was acutely aware, especially, of some bishops and priests of her time who, even in the state of grievous sin, continued to celebrate Mass and receive the Lord in the Eucharist. Her intercession for them was unceasing, but her words of rebuke to them were unsparing. As priests, they were ministers of His precious Blood. Catherine heard in her heart the Father's piercing words to a corrupted priest: "O filthy beast! I asked you to expel demons from souls and bodies by the power of the Blood whose minister I have made you, but you send them in instead."[214]

Priests like this, immersed in sin and blinded by pride, do not see that they are corrupt and on the road to perdition. And yet even to these priests who have become "devils" themselves, the Father holds out His mercy, *even* at the very moment of death: "Your only refuge will be my mercy, if you put your trust in that sweet Blood whose minister you had been made." The Father holds

---

[212] Ibid., 129, 131; p. 260, 264.
[213] Ibid., 37, 66; pp. 79, 125.
[214] Ibid., 129; p. 259.

out this same mercy to every one of us: "This last refuge will never be taken away from you or anyone else so long as you have the will to put your trust in the Blood and in my mercy."[215]

If we are bathed in the Blood of Jesus, we will go gently through death's door and find ourselves in the heart of God, "the sea of peace." Coming to the moment of our death enfolded in the Holy Spirit's comfort, we will rejoice to find ourselves "so gently brought to this passing." We will face death with trust and peace, knowing that we are immersed in and protected by the Blood of Jesus.[216]

"Oh sweet blood!" Catherine cries out. The Lord's precious Blood, which we receive in the Eucharist, deepens within us the Holy Spirit's charity, the love that brings us joy on earth and gives us entrance into Heaven's bliss.[217] And when we are blessed to enter Heaven, we will know with certainty that it is not because we are worthy of Heaven but only because we have received the Father's infinite mercy in the precious Blood of His Son.[218]

If we live every day "trusting completely in the blood of the Lamb," we will be ready even to "embrace" death "with the arms of love." Until that sacred moment, Catherine urges us to live every day bathed in the precious Blood of Jesus, whom we receive so tenderly in the Eucharist. If we do this, we will be filled with the Lord's peace in our trials and with the Holy Spirit's joy in our hearts.[219] May Catherine's wonderful counsel, example, and intercession gain for us these precious blessings through the power of the Blood of Jesus!

[215] Ibid., 129; pp. 259, 260.
[216] Ibid., 82, 131; pp. 152, 264.
[217] St. Catherine of Siena, *Letter* T 264, in *Letters*, vol. 2, p. 481.
[218] St. Catherine of Siena, *The Dialogue*, 131; p. 264.
[219] Ibid., 43; p. 89.

The Wonders of the Mass and the Eucharist

St. Teresa of Ávila

St. Teresa of Ávila (1515–1582) lived almost two centuries after St. Catherine of Siena, but they were kindred spirits. Both saints led profoundly mystical lives, even as they undertook travels on various missions of peace and reform. They were also named the first two women Doctors of the Church. Unlike Catherine, who had no schooling, Teresa was blessed to have had a superb education. Her writings were intended to give practical advice on the mystical life of prayer to her beloved Carmelite sisters. While Teresa's focus on the Eucharist is not extensive, she does give us precious advice about how to spend the time after Holy Communion treasuring the Lord's intimate presence. Like Catherine, she speaks to us with wisdom but also with her own characteristic warmth and humor.

St. Teresa of Jesus was born in Ávila, Spain, in 1515. As a young woman, she joined the Carmelite community in Ávila, but soon afterward, her health began to deteriorate, and she was paralyzed for two years. During her illness, Teresa was blessed with the grace to develop a deep life of prayer, and she then experienced a miraculous recovery. Nevertheless, after her recovery, she began to lead a mediocre and worldly religious life. After many years of living this way, she was given the grace of a profound conversion to the Lord and unswerving devotion to Him.

The Holy Spirit eventually inspired Teresa to undertake a reform that would bring back to its original purity the Carmelite convents that had become lax. Teresa received the pope's permission to open the first convent of reformed Carmelites, but her efforts were met with opposition. Nevertheless, she insisted on the nuns' living a life of enclosure, prayer, and poverty. Within a few years, the superior of the Carmelite Order asked Teresa to found even more convents of the reform. Teresa found an ally and friend in a young Carmelite priest, Juan—later known as St. John of the Cross—who initiated a corresponding reform for Carmelite men.

Even as Teresa lived a deeply mystical life, she suffered from serious health problems and endured countless trials, including constant opposition from Carmelites deeply opposed to the reform. In spite of all this, she continued her labors and travels on behalf of the Lord and was blessed to found an additional sixteen reformed convents. When Teresa was in her sixties, she found herself in the middle of a dispute between the Discalced Carmelites of the reform, who wore sandals rather than shoes, and the Calced, nonreformed, Carmelites, who wore shoes.

In the midst of this dispute, the superior of the Carmelite Order ordered Teresa to cease her reform efforts. Her beloved friend John of the Cross was even imprisoned in a nonreformed convent of the Carmelite priests. Teresa eventually obtained from the king, and then from the pope himself, recognition of the independent status of reformed Carmelite convents. As she continued her grueling schedule of travel to the reformed convents, her health problems grew worse, and, in 1582, she died on one of her journeys.

Time with the Lord after Holy Communion

Teresa was known and loved by her Carmelite sisters for her profound mystical life and for her very wise, practical way of leading them to deeper prayer. Her *Autobiography*, *The Way of Perfection*, and *The Interior Castle* are filled with profound insights on the life of prayer as well as with humor and common sense.

In *The Way of Perfection*, Teresa gives us practical advice on spending time with the Lord as our dearest Friend, especially after receiving Him in the Eucharist. As Teresa meditates on the Our Father, she is struck by the beautiful petition "Give us this daily bread." This is not a request for created food, Teresa assures us, but a request for the Lord Himself: "The good Jesus, being ours, asks His Father to let us have *Him* daily." We can have Him every day if we want, for He has chosen in love to *stay* with us, giving Himself to us even as our Food. This is such a tremendous joy and comfort for us: that we can have the Lord physically within us every day in the Eucharist if we want![220] Those who saw the Lord when He visibly walked this earth had no advantage over us, Teresa tells us. In the Eucharist, the Lord is not only *with* us, as He was with them; even more deeply, in the Eucharist, He is *within* us as our Food.[221]

The Eucharistic Lord is not only our Food but is also *healing* for our bodies as well as our souls. Surely speaking of herself, Teresa tells us that she knows someone who often suffered from serious illnesses and who was in constant pain. But through the Lord's wonderful responses to her fervent prayer after Holy Communion, her pain "was taken away from her in a flash, and she became quite well again." Teresa tells us that she believes that physical healing "often" is granted to those who receive the Lord in Holy Communion and that these marvelous blessings of the Eucharistic Lord bestowed on us are "very well known."[222]

To help her focus her own attention completely on the Lord after receiving Holy Communion, Teresa would sometimes picture the Lord entering her home, or she would imagine that she was with Mary Magdalene as she washed His feet with her tears. Picturing the Lord in this way after receiving Him in the Eucharist is not like picturing Him at other times, Teresa tells us. The Lord does dwell within us through sanctifying grace, but when we receive Him

---

[220] St. Teresa of Ávila, *The Way of Perfection*, chap. 34, p. 105.
[221] Ibid., p. 106.
[222] Ibid.

in Holy Communion, He is *physically* within us. "It is absolutely *true*, and we have no need to go and seek Him somewhere a long way off." After Holy Communion, we are not simply "picturing" the Lord with and within us; "the good Jesus" *is* with and within us. And even when she *felt* no devotion, Teresa tells us, she would simply rest with the Lord, for she knew through faith that it was "good" for her to be there (Matt. 17:4).[223] Indeed, after we receive the Lord, we have Heaven itself within us, for the *Lord* of Heaven is within us.[224]

Teresa offers us a beautiful meditation on why the Lord does not permit us to see Him with our physical eyes. Our human nature is so weak that we could not bear the sight of Him in His risen glory, she tells us. How could we who are weak and prone to sin bear to "remain so near to Him"? With our imperfections, with our meager faith and love, we would never dare even to approach Him. Ah, but when He "hides" and "disguises Himself" under the ordinary species of bread and wine, Teresa assures us, we are not afraid to be with Him and to be so close to Him.[225]

Let us then "*delight* to *remain* with Him." Teresa stresses that the time after Holy Communion is so precious because it is a time to speak heart to heart with the Lord. The blessings for us are infinite, for we are "in the company of the good Jesus," the Lord of Heaven and earth. If a pressing responsibility calls us away after we have received the Lord, let us at least try to stay with Him in our *hearts*. Teresa urges us not to receive the Lord and then neglect Him by letting our thoughts wander a million miles away. The Lord has so

---

[223] Ibid., chap. 34, p. 106.
[224] Ibid., chap. 29, p. 91.
[225] Ibid., chap. 34, p. 106.

much to give us, but if we care nothing about His presence, how can He shower on us His intimate love?[226]

After receiving Holy Communion, let us simply *be* with Jesus our Lord and not worry about many words. He wants to love and comfort and strengthen us, and He has "no wish for us to tire our brains by a great deal of talking."[227] The Lord may draw us simply to rest on His heart, as the beloved disciple did at the Last Supper (John 13:23). Or the Holy Spirit may place a few words in our hearts, such as those we find in the Gospels: "Lord, you know that I love You" (John 21:17); "Lord, be merciful to me, a sinner" (Luke 18:13); "My Lord and my God!" (John 20:28).

Regardless of how the Holy Spirit draws us to pray after Holy Communion, let us beg the Lord never to leave us. During the day, it may help us to pray while gazing at a tender picture of the Lord, perhaps on the Cross. But when we have received the Lord Himself in Holy Communion and are in His intimate presence, let us simply close our eyes and, with the eyes of faith, look at *Him* dwelling within us. How foolish it would be, Teresa remarks, if we had a picture of someone dear to us but when he came to visit us, "we refused to talk with him and carried on our entire conversation with the portrait?"[228]

We cannot physically see the Lord, but He is our dearest Friend. When we invite our friends to our home, we don't insult them by completely ignoring them. As cherished friends of the Lord, Teresa tells us, let us prepare our hearts to receive Him. But let us not then insult Him by thinking of other things after we have received Him into the home of our hearts. And let us

---

[226] Ibid.

[227] Ibid., chap. 29, p. 91.

[228] Ibid., chap. 34, p. 107.

not rush out immediately after Mass to attend to more important matters![229]

Teresa reminds us that when the Lord walked this earth, He worked miracles of love and healing for those who came to Him. Sick people were healed when they simply touched His clothes. How can we doubt that the same Lord Jesus will work miracles of love and healing for *us* after we receive Him in the Eucharist? He surely "will give us what we ask of Him since He *is in our house*." When we have the privilege of receiving the Lord in the Eucharist, let us truly *spend time* with Him and show Him that we love to be with Him![230]

Teresa asks us to picture a great fire ready to warm us on a bitterly cold night. She reminds us that we need to stay close to the fire for more than just a few seconds if we want to benefit from its heat. So, too, let us *stay* with the Lord after Holy Communion so that we may be truly warmed by the fire of His love. Teresa concludes her reflections by reminding us of how sweet it is to have in our home the lingering fragrance of a beloved friend who has just visited us. Let us, then, give our heart's love and attention to the Lord after receiving Him in Holy Communion and *continue* to enjoy throughout the day the warmth and fragrance of His love within us.[231]

May Teresa's wise counsels help us to cherish more deeply the Lord's gift of Himself to us in the Eucharist. Through her intercession, may the soul of each one of us become more truly the home where the Lord is always welcomed, loved, and treasured.

---

[229] Ibid.
[230] Ibid., p. 106.
[231] Ibid., chap. 35, p. 109

5

St. Elizabeth Ann Seton and
St. John Henry Newman

Longing for the Lord in the Eucharist

In this chapter, we consider two marvelous saints who were converts to the Catholic Faith and great lovers of the Lord in the Eucharist: St. Elizabeth Ann Seton and St. John Henry Newman.

St. Elizabeth Ann Seton

St. Elizabeth Ann Bayley Seton (1774–1821) stands out among the saints for the intimate account she gives us of her difficult journey to the Catholic Faith and her deepening hunger for the Lord in the Eucharist. Elizabeth Bayley was a devout Episcopalian from a prominent New York family. When she was twenty, she fell deeply in love with and married William Seton, a wealthy New York business-man, with whom she had five children. They were married not yet ten years when William's business transactions began to fail. At the same time, he began suffering from tuberculosis, which would also afflict other members of his family and, eventually, Elizabeth herself.

William's doctor advised him to spend time in Italy, in the hope that the warm weather would help bring him back to good health. He and Elizabeth made the difficult decision to journey to

The Wonders of the Mass and the Eucharist

Italy with their oldest daughter, Anna Maria, leaving four children at home in the care of a loving woman who worked for them.

Soon after their arrival in December 1803, William's illness grew worse. Within a short time, he died, unaware of his business failures and believing that he had provided well for his beloved wife and children. In fact, however, Elizabeth was left penniless. Before she and Anna Maria could return to New York, they both became ill. William's business associates in Italy, the deeply Catholic Filicchi family, generously invited Elizabeth and Anna Maria to stay with them in their home in Livorno, called by the English "Leghorn."

Over the next several months, the Filicchis lovingly cared for Elizabeth and Anna Maria, becoming dear friends with them and including them in every aspect of their lives, especially their deeply Catholic devotions. As she accompanied the Filicchis to Mass, Elizabeth began to be affected by the profound worship that filled the church, especially at the Consecration. Increasingly, she found herself drawn to the mystery and beauty of the Catholic belief in the Real Presence of the Lord in the Eucharist.

Elizabeth was able to return to New York in June 1804. Even as she resumed her religious practices as a fervent Episcopalian, however, she could not shake her attraction to the Mass and the Eucharist. And yet she also was plagued by doubts and influenced by disparaging comments made by her Episcopalian friends about the Catholic Faith. As a devoted Episcopalian, Elizabeth loved going to the service of Holy Communion, which she considered to be very holy. Her Episcopal faith had taught her, however, that Holy Communion is not the actual Body and Blood of the Lord.

After spending almost a year in agonizing prayer and study and seeking the counsel of trusted Catholic friends, Elizabeth made the life-changing decision to become a Catholic. In March 1805, she was received into the Catholic Church. This wonderful event brought her tremendous joy and peace of soul, but it also increased her trials, as dear Episcopalian friends turned against her. Elizabeth's sorrows were intensified when her beloved sister-in-law, Rebecca, the friend of her soul who shared her deep attraction to the Catholic Faith, died of tuberculosis.

For the next several years, Elizabeth endured further financial, emotional, and physical trials. By 1807, however, she had become more well known in Catholic circles, especially as a woman who was a gifted teacher. In 1808, the Holy Spirit inspired Elizabeth to accept an invitation from the Sulpician president of St. Mary's College, Fr. Louis William DuBourg, to open a Catholic school for girls in Baltimore. The Sulpicians helped to recruit others to join Elizabeth in her work, and under her leadership, a new American religious congregation was formed. In June 1809, Elizabeth and four young women professed vows before Bishop John Carroll of Baltimore. Within several months, they moved to Emmitsburg, Maryland, where they began their religious life as Sisters of Charity of St. Joseph's and soon opened St. Joseph Free School for Girls, the first free Catholic school in the United States.

Elizabeth became the first superior of the new community, a responsibility that she held for the next twelve years. But life was not easy for her. During her time at Emmitsburg, with gentleness of spirit and tenderness of heart, she endured further trials, including the heartbreaking deaths of two of her daughters to tuberculosis. Eventually, Elizabeth herself contracted tuberculosis and died in 1821, at the age of forty-six. In 1975, Pope St. Paul VI canonized Elizabeth Ann Bayley Seton as the first native-born saint of the United States.

Elizabeth Seton's Attraction to the Eucharist

Elizabeth's journal and her letters to her beloved sister-in-law Rebecca Seton are treasured because they give us an intimate account of Elizabeth's fervor as an Episcopalian, the great trials and blessings of her time in Italy, and her growing attraction to the Catholic Faith, especially to the Eucharist. She describes the sorrow of the declining health of her husband, William, and how much she longed for the comfort of attending Episcopal services of Holy Communion with him and all her children. Anna Maria was with them, but Elizabeth sorely missed her other children and was comforted by the thought that she could be with them in spirit as they attended services in New York.

As William rapidly grew more ill, Elizabeth stayed constantly by his bedside. She prayed the Episcopal Communion Service with him, longing to receive the Episcopal "cup of Thanksgiving" with him in the "strange land" of Italy.[232] Deprived of human companionship in her agony, Elizabeth was consoled by her faith that the Lord was with her as she prayed beside William, doing all that she could to relieve his pain.[233]

In her journal entries to Rebecca, we see Elizabeth's ardent love for her beloved William and their fervent love for the Lord. Though suffering excruciating pain, William endured it with gratitude to the Lord and love for his "darling" children as they began to celebrate Christmas, the "day that opened to us the door of everlasting life." Knowing how near he was to death, William longed to receive the "Sacrament" a final time, and Elizabeth did all she could to make that possible. She put wine in a glass, said psalms and prayers, and, together with William, "took the cup of Thanksgiving." On her

---

[232] St. Elizabeth Seton, Journal to Rebecca Seton, 2.7, in Elizabeth Ann Seton, *Collected Writings*, vol. 1, pt. 2, ed. Regina Bechtle, S.C., and Judith Metz, S.C. (New York: New City Press, 2000), p. 266.

[233] Ibid., pp. 267, 268, 270.

knees by his bedside, Elizabeth begged the Lord to free her dear William from his sufferings, as he himself would keep praying, "I want to be in Heaven, pray, pray, for my Soul"; "My dear Wife and little ones"; "My Christ Jesus, have mercy and receive me." On December 27, William peacefully died.[234]

As the law required, within the next twenty-four hours, he was buried, in the graveyard of the Anglican Church in Leghorn. We can only imagine Elizabeth's profound grief over his death and her sorrow that she would have to leave the body of her beloved William in a grave in Italy. She was comforted, however, that the Lord had taken him home before he could realize the family's dire financial condition. Elizabeth also received immense consolation from the tremendous kindnesses of William's business partners in Italy, the Filicchi family. They took her and Anna Maria into their home, showed them every possible kindness, and treated them as beloved family members.[235]

On Sunday, January 8, 1804, Elizabeth attended her first Mass with Mrs. Amabilia Filicchi. She was transfixed by the experience. The sight of hundreds of people on their knees, filled with silent worship, overwhelmed her. Elizabeth was so moved by the "heavenly" music and the warmth of the candlelight that, oblivious to everything else, she herself sank to her knees and wept a "torrent of tears." In her heart, she sorely missed her own church in New York, and she prayed as much as she could remember of her beloved Episcopal service. After Mass, she and Mrs. Filicchi walked around the chapel. Its beauty, Elizabeth notes, was impossible to describe. She was profoundly moved by the sight of "all sorts of

---

[234] Ibid., pp. 273, 274.
[235] St. Elizabeth Seton, Letter to Rebecca Seton, 2.8; in *Collected Writings*, vol. 1, pt. 2, p. 278.

people kneeling ... about the Altar as inattentive to us or any other passengers, as if we were not there."[236]

A month later, Elizabeth wrote of going to Mass again with Mrs. Filicchi and of being absolutely overcome with emotion when she was told that the *Lord Himself* was truly present in the church. "I don't know how to say the awful effect at being where they told me *God* was present in the Blessed Sacrament." Filled with "such strange impressions," she could only put her face in her hands and "let the tears run." "Oh my," Elizabeth cried out, "the very little while we were there will never be forgotten though I saw nothing and no one."[237]

A few days later, Elizabeth wrote to her "dearest" Rebecca about an upsetting conversation with Mr. Antonio Filicchi in which she asked him what he thought about the beliefs of various religions. He responded that there is only "one true Religion." But what about all those who don't believe in that "one true religion," Elizabeth asked. Filicchi didn't know about that, but he did know "where people will go who *can* know the right Faith if they pray for it and enquire for it, and yet do neither." Elizabeth was so amused by his obvious attempt to lure her to the Catholic Faith that she laughed out loud. He asked her only to pray and inquire. "Laughing with God," Elizabeth did pray daily the prayer, "If I am right, O teach my heart still in the right to stay; if I am wrong thy grace impart to find the better way." In no way did Elizabeth think that there *was* a better way than her own Episcopalian faith. And yet, she thought, surely every faith, including the Catholic Faith, should be respected.[238]

---

[236] St. Elizabeth Seton, Florence Journal to Rebecca Seton, 2.10, in *Collected Writings*, vol. 1, pt. 2, pp. 283, 284.

[237] St. Elizabeth Seton, Letter to Rebecca Seton, 2.11, in *Collected Writings*, vol. 1, pt. 2, pp. 289, 290.

[238] Ibid., 290.

In spite of her profound Episcopal convictions, Elizabeth describes how disturbed she was at another Mass she attended. A young Englishman, at the "very moment the Priest was doing the most sacred action they call the Elevation," explained *loudly* to her that this is what Catholics believe to be the "real PRESENCE." "My very heart trembled with shame and sorrow for his unfeeling interruption of their sacred adoration, for all around was dead Silence and many were prostrated."[239]

What Elizabeth says next is telling. "Involuntarily *I* bent from him to the pavement and thought secretly on the word of St. Paul with starting tears, 'they discern not the Lord's body'" (1 Cor. 11:29). And then it struck Elizabeth: How can people be blamed for failing to discern the *Lord's body* "if indeed *it is not there?*" Doubts began to fill her, doubts about *how* the *Lord Himself* can be present in the Eucharist, doubts about "a hundred other things." She firmly believed that God the Son truly became human in His mother's womb, and *yet*, as a mother, she wondered, *how* could *this*, also, be true: "How was my GOD a little babe in the first stage of his mortal existence in Mary?" Her doubts and musings, Elizabeth wrote to Rebecca, were absorbed into the greater longing she was feeling to be with her little ones whom she had left behind in New York.[240]

In the "strange but beautiful land" of Italy, Elizabeth's heart was beginning to long for more than her children. "How happy we would be if we believed what these dear souls believe," she wrote to Rebecca, "that they possess *God* in the Sacrament and that he remains in their churches" and is even brought to the sick. Elizabeth recounts how, whenever the Blessed Sacrament was

---

[239] Ibid., 291.
[240] Ibid.

carried in procession under her window, her heart would be so deeply touched that she would *weep*. Comforted by the presence of a chapel even in the Filicchis' home, Elizabeth cries out, "My God, how happy would I be even so far away from all so dear, if I could find *You* in the church as *they* do." Overcome with grief over the death of her beloved husband and her separation from the rest of her children, in a "moment of excessive distress" and without thinking, she fell on her knees as the Blessed Sacrament was carried past her in procession. "I . . . cried in an agony to God to bless me *if he was there*," for "my whole Soul desired only Him."[241]

One day, Elizabeth took up a small prayer book of Mrs. Filicchi's and opened it to the Memorare. Having suffered the death of her own mother when she was only three years old, Elizabeth begged our Blessed Mother to help her in her sorrows, trusting that the Lord would refuse no request that His own Mother made to Him. As she prayed, Elizabeth's heart was filled with the most tender comfort and peace. "I felt really that I had a *Mother*, which, you know, my foolish heart so often lamented to have lost." Indeed, all her life she had longed for her mother. "At that moment it seemed as if I had found *more* than her, even in the tenderness and pity of a Mother. I cried myself to sleep in her heart."[242]

As the weeks passed by, Elizabeth wrote to Rebecca about how much Catholic practices and devotions were beginning to affect her. One day, Antonio Filicchi taught her to make the Sign of the Cross. "Dearest Rebecca, I was cold with the awful impression my first making it gave me. The Sign of the CROSS of Christ on *me*." As she made the Sign of the Cross, "deepest thoughts came

---

[241] Ibid., pp. 292, 293.
[242] Ibid., p. 293.

with it … earnest desires to be closely united with him who died on it." Other Catholic practices began to draw her heart. During Lent, Mrs. Filicchi fasted until the late afternoon meal, offering her fasting as well as her own physical pains to the Lord, who suffered so intensely on the Cross for us. "I like that very much," Elizabeth wrote. Best of all, Elizabeth was touched by this tremendous "comfort:" "they go to Mass here *every morning.*"[243]

When she had been in New York, every Sunday evening Elizabeth would leave the Episcopalian service arm in arm with Rebecca and feel bereft that they had to wait until the next Sunday to go again. "Well, *here* they go to church at 4 *every* morning if they please!" Elizabeth also recalls how, on every "Sacrament Sunday," held then six times a year, she and Rebecca would go from Episcopal church to church so that they could receive Communion as often as possible. "Well, *here* people that love God and live a good regular life can go (tho' many do not do it) yet they *can* go *every day!*" "O my," Elizabeth cries out, "I don't know how anybody can have any trouble in this world who believes all these dear souls believe. If I don't believe it, it shall not be for want of praying." Because they are blessed with these precious gifts, Elizabeth believed that Catholics must be as happy "as the angels almost."[244]

Elizabeth's young daughter, Anna Maria, "wild with joy," often asked if they could *please* attend a *Catholic* church when they got back to New York. The child had grown to love Mrs. Filicchi's practice of stopping to pray in Catholic churches when they would take a walk together. Elizabeth grew to love that practice. When she and Anna Maria would go for a walk, they made sure that they

[243] St. Elizabeth Seton, Journal to Rebecca Seton, 2.14, in *Collected Writings*, vol. 1, pt. 2, pp. 296, 297.

[244] Ibid., p. 297.

would stop along the way for a visit to a Catholic church and spend time in prayer before the Blessed Sacrament.[245]

Elizabeth was deeply touched to see not only women but also men stopping in church to pray before the Blessed Sacrament. In her Episcopal church in New York, she recalled, men would be embarrassed to be found kneeling or visiting the church, especially during the week. And yet, even as she enjoyed a newfound peace, she also struggled with anxiety about where her "home" really would be in the midst of the sorrow and destitution she was suffering. Antonio Filicchi assured her, "My little sister, God, the Almighty, is laughing at you. He takes care of little birds.... He will take care of you."[246]

When it was finally time for Elizabeth and Anna Maria to return to New York, they were accompanied by Antonio, who had business to attend to in America and who lovingly insisted on accompanying them on the journey. Before going to the ship, they all attended Mass together, during which Elizabeth prayed fervently for all her loved ones. But she was especially struck by the profound devotion with which the Filicchis received the Lord in Holy Communion together. She became even more keenly aware of her own deepening desire to partake of that same "blessed body and blood."

Arriving in New York in June 1804, Elizabeth was ecstatic to be reunited with the rest of her children. She discovered, however, that Rebecca, the beloved companion and sister of her soul, was suffering from tuberculosis and did not have long to live. After the death of her husband and the loss of close friends, home, and financial resources, Elizabeth was devastated to face the loss of

[245] Ibid.
[246] Ibid., pp. 297, 298.

this, her intimate friend in her every trial. She begged the Lord for the grace to experience these, her many sufferings, as her "dearest friends."[247]

Elizabeth continued to correspond with Antonio Filicchi when he returned to Italy. She followed his advice to start adopting various Catholic practices, such as reading the lives of the saints, a devotion that Elizabeth grew to enjoy very much. When she read about saints, such as Augustine, who experienced doubts and struggles in their own conversions to the Lord, she was especially comforted and encouraged to trust that the Lord would find a way to bring her, also, to her true "Home."[248]

And yet Elizabeth could not completely free herself from the doubts that plagued her: "Antonio, Antonio, why cannot my poor Soul be satisfied that your religion is now the same that *theirs* then was. How can it hesitate? Why must it struggle? The Almighty only can decide." In another letter to Antonio, she cries out, "O my Brother! ... If you could know the shocking and awful objects presented to my mind in *opposition* to your Church, you would say it is impossible except a voice from Heaven directed, that I *ever* could become a member of it."[249]

In a draft letter to Antonio's brother, Filippo Filicchi, Elizabeth wrote, "For some months, I have stood between the two ways ... often in the Protestant Church [but] finding my Soul at Mass in Leghorn." As a help to arriving at a firm decision,

---

[247] Ibid., pp. 298, 299; St. Elizabeth Seton, Journal to Rebecca Seton, 3.1, in *Collected Writings*, vol. 1, pt. 3, p. 308.

[248] St. Elizabeth Seton, Letter to Antonio Filicchi, 3.9, in *Collected Writings*, vol. 1, pt. 3, p. 325.

[249] Ibid.; St. Elizabeth Seton, Letter to Antonio Filicchi, 3.15, in *Collected Writings*, vol. 1, pt. 3, p. 339.

Elizabeth resolved to continue reading books on the Catholic Faith.[250] And in a journal to Amabilia Filicchi, she made an intimate confession. As Elizabeth faithfully attended services at her own Episcopal church, she nevertheless would find a pew that would allow her to look upon the *Catholic* church nearby. "I found myself twenty times speaking to the Blessed Sacrament *there* instead of looking at the naked altar where I was." Throughout her own Episcopal service, Elizabeth would quietly weep with longing for the Eucharist in the Catholic church. When a friend asked her how she could possibly believe what Catholics believe, and especially that the Lord is truly present in the Blessed Sacrament in every Catholic Church and chapel throughout the world, Elizabeth smiled and thought to herself: "It is GOD who does it, the same God who fed so many thousands with the little barley loaves and little fishes."[251]

Elizabeth found that she was being drawn by a deep attraction to the "heavenly consolations" of the Lord's presence in the Blessed Sacrament. This infinitely precious gift could *not* be of human making, she reasoned. Surely, the Lord, who filled the Ark of the Old Covenant with His presence, would not be so uncaring about *our* happiness today as to "leave our churches with nothing but naked walls and our altars unadorned." A friend had told Elizabeth that she did not believe what Catholics believe, but she did find Catholic beliefs to be comforting and *wished* she could share them. Elizabeth admitted that Catholic beliefs were beginning to be of tremendous comfort to *her* in her own trials and sufferings,

---

[250] St. Elizabeth Seton, Draft Letter to Filippo Filicchi, 3.17, in *Collected Writings*, vol. 1, pt. 3, pp. 341, 342.

[251] St. Elizabeth Seton, Journal to Amabilia Filicchi, 3.31, in *Collected Writings*, vol. 1, pt. 3, p. 370.

which sometimes were so devastating that she wondered if she would die of them.[252]

In a letter to Amabilia Filicchi, Elizabeth recounted how her Episcopal friends were bombarding her with attacks against Catholics, whom they considered to be society's "offscourings." And Catholic churches are "a public Nuisance"! Elizabeth confessed that, in "desperation of heart," she went to her Episcopal church, "looked straight up to God," and told the Lord that she wanted only to please Him, but she *did not know* what He wanted of her. Until He clearly showed her His will for her, she would *stay* in the Episcopal church: "I will trudge on in the path you suffered me to be born in, and go even to the very sacrament where I once *used* to find you." But Elizabeth found it impossible to do what she intended. "If I left the house a Protestant, I returned to it a Catholic." She could no longer fight her attraction to the Catholic Faith. "I determined to go no more to the Protestants, being much more troubled than ever I thought I could be."[253]

Most of all, receiving Communion in her church deeply troubled Elizabeth. The proclamation, "the Body and Blood of Christ," was qualified by the words "*spiritually* taken and received." And yet the service was addressed to the Lord "really present." Elizabeth became "half crazy" by the contradiction. She decided to abandon everything into the Lord's hands and to entrust her life to our Blessed Mother's care. Elizabeth had become convinced that, for her peace of soul, she *had* to go to the church where, she was now convinced, "true Faith" *first began*. She *had* to go to "those who received it from *God Himself*." Elizabeth's resolve now was utterly

---

[252] Ibid., pp. 370, 372.
[253] Ibid., p. 373.

firm. "To the *Catholics* I will go, and try to be a good one.... May God accept my intention and pity me." [254]

Elizabeth confessed to Amabilia that she found herself alternately laughing and crying. But she was not at all afraid. "I trust all to God. It is his Affair now." On March 14, 1805, at St. Peter's Catholic Church in New York City, Elizabeth made her profession of faith as a Catholic. Her first confession soon afterward was for her a tremendous "unloosing after a 30 years' bondage. I felt as if my chains fell." Now, with immense longing, Elizabeth began to "count the days and hours" when she could receive her First Holy Communion. [255]

Elizabeth describes to Amabilia the sleepless vigil she kept the night before her First Holy Communion. It was a night filled with the most intense anticipation and longing. In the morning, every step she took brought her nearer to her heart's desire, the moment when her King would come to "take up His throne" within her soul. On the feast of the Annunciation, March 25, 1805, Elizabeth received the Lord in the Eucharist for the first time. Of this momentous grace, she wrote, "*At last*, God is mine and I am His. I have *received* Him." And her heart "danced" with joy! *Finally*, the Lord in all His glory and love, had come to *her*, giving her, through the most intimate love for her, His own precious Body and Blood, making her, body and soul, His "little poor Kingdom." [256]

As she reflected on this most intimate grace and immense privilege of receiving the Lord, Elizabeth wrote to Amabilia that, overcome with awe and worship, she could only cry out in her soul, over and over, "*My God* is *here*." With the apostle St. Thomas,

---

[254] Ibid., pp. 373, 374.
[255] Ibid., pp. 374, 375, 376.
[256] Ibid., pp. 376, 377.

her heart cried out to the Lord truly within her, "My Lord and my God!" (John 20:28). Elizabeth comments that she absolutely could *not* understand how *any* Catholics could willingly deprive themselves of the wondrous gifts of the Mass and the Eucharist. Even though she herself was plagued with severe health problems and trials of every kind, Elizabeth was also filled with immense gratitude and "unspeakable joy and reverence" before these Sacred Mysteries and prayed for the grace to attend Mass every day if she could.[257]

Elizabeth continued to endure other trials, including suffering dire poverty and not knowing how she would feed and care for her children. Abandoned by friends, she felt she had nowhere to turn for help. And yet her soul was filled with contentment, for in the Blessed Sacrament, she fed on the Lord Himself and tasted the very joys of Heaven.[258]

The intense love for the Eucharist that filled Elizabeth's heart deepened through the years. In her journal to her sister-in-law Cecilia Seton, written two years after her conversion, Elizabeth recounts her increasingly intimate love for the Sacrament of the Lord's precious Body and Blood. She tells of the "sweetness" of the Lord's presence filling her soul and of how moved she was by the inestimable gift of receiving the *Lord Himself* into her inmost being. "This Bread of Angels removes my pain, my cares ... warms, cheers, soothes, contents and renews my whole being." No tongue could express the "Treasure of Peace and contentment" that the intimate presence of her Lord and God, the "Kindest, tenderest, dearest Friend," gave her. The tremendous gift of the Lord's

[257] Ibid., p. 378.
[258] St. Elizabeth Seton, Letter to Amabilia Filicchi, 3.24, in *Collected Writings*, vol. 1, pt. 3, p. 353.

intimate presence drew her to have His sacred name always in her heart and on her lips. The precious name of Jesus, whom we so intimately receive in the Sacred Sacrament, is the "antidote to all the discord that surrounds us," she writes.[259]

Profoundly aware of how blessed she was to be in the Lord's intimate physical presence at Mass and to taste His sweetness in the Eucharist, Elizabeth began to grieve for all those who do not know the sacred gift of the Lord's Precious Body and Blood. Not blessed to enjoy the Lord's Real Presence in the Sacrament of the Eucharist, they have services "founded on Words" from which they take only "the Shadow." In contrast, those blessed to attend Mass and to receive the Eucharist enjoy the *Lord Himself* in the very "center" of their souls. Yes, surely the Lord is everywhere, she writes, but in the Sacrament of the Eucharist, He is "as present *actually* and *really* as my Soul within my Body." And, in the Sacrifice of the Mass, *every day* He is offered as truly as He was offered long ago on the Cross. "Merciful Saviour!" Elizabeth cries out. "Can there be *any* comparison to this Blessedness?" "Adored Lord," she prays, "*keep* me in thy sweet pastures and lead me to Eternal Life."[260]

In a letter to Antonio Filicchi written three years after her reception into the Catholic Church, Elizabeth describes how blessed she was to be able to attend Mass and receive the Lord in the Eucharist almost every day.[261] She had moved to Baltimore at the invitation of Fr. William DuBourg, and Bishop John Carroll had recommended her to Catholic parents as a superb teacher to

---

[259] St. Elizabeth Seton, Spiritual Journal to Cecilia Seton, 4.55, in *Collected Writings*, vol. 1, pt. 4, pp. 477, 478.

[260] Ibid., pp. 478, 479.

[261] St. Elizabeth Seton, Letter to Antonio Filicchi 5.14, in *Collected Writings*, vol. 2, pt. 5, ed. Regina Bechtle, S.C. and Judith Metz, S.C. (New York: New City Press, 2002), p. 45.

prepare their children for their First Holy Communion. Elizabeth loved her work with these children and felt deeply privileged to spend time in the chapel beside the home in which she lived. She recounts how the chapel was filled with the most tender love and adoration in celebration of the "heavenly day" when several young girls received their First Holy Communion.[262]

Elizabeth also describes with intense emotion how deeply she was touched by a Mass celebrated by a priest in the lower chapel of St. Mary's Church in Baltimore. The celebrant himself *wept* as he gave the Sacrament of the Eucharist to those present, and "we had liberty to sob aloud unwitnessed by any." Another precious grace for Elizabeth was being present at Benediction of the Blessed Sacrament in the Church of St. Mary's in Baltimore. Surrounded by devout priests and seminarians, drinking in the beauty of the hymns, deeply moved by the adoration that filled the church, Elizabeth felt the presence of the Lord Himself, as if gathered with His own beloved apostles.[263]

Four years after her conversion, Elizabeth wrote to her dear friend Antonio Filicchi about how tremendously happy she was preparing children for their First Holy Communion. She recalls with profound gratitude how her resistance to becoming a Catholic had been conquered by the "overwhelming power" of "the divine Light of Faith." It was through faith that she truly could "see and taste its infinite sweetness."[264]

Surely, the Mass and the Eucharist are the most precious "sweetness" of the Catholic Faith which Elizabeth was blessed to discover.

---

[262] St. Elizabeth Seton, Letter to Cecilia Seton, 5.22, in *Collected Writings*, vol. 2, pt. 5, p. 64.

[263] Ibid., p. 65.

[264] St. Elizabeth Seton, Letter to Antonio Filicchi, 5.14, in *Collected Writings*, vol. 2, pt. 5, p. 46.

The Wonders of the Mass and the Eucharist

May Elizabeth obtain for us the grace of a deeper desire in our own hearts to be present at Mass and to receive the precious Body and Blood of the Lord in the Eucharist as often as possible.

St. John Henry Newman

Born twenty years before Elizabeth Seton's death, St. John Henry Newman (1801–1890) was an esteemed scholar and devout Anglican priest whom the Holy Spirit also drew to the Catholic Faith. As a young man, Newman attended Trinity College at Oxford and then was elected as a fellow at Oriel College, Oxford, a position he held from 1822 to 1845. Ordained an Anglican priest, he served as chaplain at Oriel, where students and colleagues became his dear friends. For seventeen years, he also ministered as vicar at the Oxford University Church of St. Mary's, whose congregation deeply loved him. His eloquent sermons, spoken in a quiet voice and with profound recollection, touched the minds and hearts of the many people who came to hear him.

The Holy Spirit inspired in Newman a growing desire to work for the renewal of the Church of England by studying and illuminating what he believed were its roots in the early Church. For him, the Anglican church held a privileged place as the "middle way" between the seeming extremes of Catholicism and evangelical Protestantism. With dear friends of like mind, Newman initiated the Oxford Movement, publishing pamphlets, or tracts, on topics related to their hoped-for renewal. These tracts became so popular that they aroused growing suspicion and opposition from Anglican colleagues and friends who believed that Newman was betraying the Anglican tradition by becoming too "Catholic." In fact, Newman *was* being drawn to the Catholic Faith. Far from nurturing an animosity toward Catholic beliefs like many of his colleagues, Newman became increasingly sympathetic toward the

Catholic Faith. He later wrote that the influence of dear friends such as Hurrell Froude had caused him to "look with admiration towards the Church of Rome" and had even led him to believe in the Real Presence of the Lord in the Eucharist.[265]

Through his intense study of the Church Fathers, Newman grew to realize that he could not identify the roots of the Church of England in the early Church. After profound study and prayer, he made the heartrending decision to leave his beloved Oxford and move to the nearby village of Littlemore. Close friends, including students and colleagues at Oxford, went with him, and together they undertook a quiet life of asceticism, prayer, and study. Within two years, in 1845, Newman published his *Essay on the Development of Christian Doctrine*, showing that Catholic beliefs that could seem to be additions to Scripture are, in fact, living doctrines that are organic developments from Scripture. That same year, on October 9, 1845, Newman was received into the Catholic Church.

Even though the Holy Spirit also drew some faithful friends of his to become Catholic, Newman's decision cost him dearly. Other friends, family, and revered colleagues abandoned him and turned against him. Surely referring to this very painful time, Newman later wrote that he placed all his trust in the Lord, who, he believed, had entrusted to him a work "not committed to another." "He may take away my friends ... make my spirits sink, hide the future from me—still He knows what He is about."[266] Newman's conversion to the Catholic Church, though accompanied by severe

---

[265] St. John Henry Newman, *Apologia pro Vita Sua* (London: Longmans, Green, 1908), chap. 1, p. 25.

[266] St. John Henry Newman, "Meditations on Christian Doctrine," 2, 3, in *Meditations and Devotions*, ed. W. P. Neville (London: Longmans, Green, 1907), pp. 301, 302.

trials, also brought him tremendous peace. He later wrote, "From the time that I became a Catholic.... I have been in perfect peace and contentment; I never have had one doubt." Rather than regretting his decision, Newman found that becoming a Catholic "was like coming into port after a rough sea; and my happiness on that score remains to this day without interruption."[267]

A special gift that the Holy Spirit gave to Newman was believing with untroubled mind all the articles of faith taught by the Catholic Church. "I made a profession of them upon my reception with the greatest ease, and I have the same ease in believing them now," he later wrote. Newman notes that, before he became a Catholic, he did not believe the Catholic doctrine of transubstantiation — the belief that, at the Consecration of the Mass, the Lord, through the ministry of the bishop or priest, transforms the entire substance of the bread and wine into His precious Body and Blood. However, as soon as Newman was given the grace to believe that the teachings of the Catholic Church are the truth revealed by God, he had absolutely "no difficulty" in believing the Catholic teaching about the Eucharist.[268]

Two years after his conversion, and following upon studies in Rome, Newman was ordained a Catholic priest there. While studying at Rome, he came to know and admire the sixteenth-century St. Philip Neri and his Congregation of the Oratory, small communities of priests bound together by love and dedicated to ministry in the world. A year later, Newman received papal permission to establish the Oratory of St. Philip Neri in Birmingham, England. There, the small group would minister to the many poor members of the local church to which the community was attached.

---

[267] St. John Henry Newman, *Apologia pro Vita Sua*, chap. 5, p. 238.
[268] Ibid.

In 1851, Newman was invited to help found the Catholic University of Ireland, now known as University College, Dublin. The university opened in 1854, and Newman served as rector there for several years, with varying degrees of success. In 1858, he resigned to devote his attention to his cherished Oratory in Birmingham. For the rest of his life, Newman remained committed to and tremendously grateful for his brother priests of the Oratory, who, throughout the years, were a constant source of strength and comfort to him in all his trials.[269]

Newman's sermons and writings as a Catholic priest and scholar were marked by profound insight, grace, and beauty. Not everyone was pleased, however, with what he wrote. He had suffered the enmity of Anglican colleagues and friends. Now, though he was honored and supported by some distinguished members of the Catholic clergy, he was looked upon with disdain by others.

Throughout the trials of his life, however, Newman had been blessed for more than thirty years by the close friendship and support of fellow convert, scholar, and brother Oratorian Ambrose St. John. Four years after the death of Ambrose, Newman's Catholic orthodoxy was vindicated when, in 1879, Pope Leo XIII named him a cardinal of the Catholic Church. Newman continued his labors of prayer, preaching, and writing at his beloved Oratory at Birmingham. All the while, through his abundant correspondence and wise counsel, he graciously and generously helped the many people who sought his spiritual guidance. In 1890, Newman died at the age of eighty-nine. He had become so well known and loved that large crowds lined the streets of Birmingham to honor him as his funeral procession passed by.

[269] Ibid., p. 283.

The Wonders of the Mass and the Eucharist

In the Mass, the Lord Makes Present His Saving Death

As a Catholic, Newman treasured the Eucharist with all his soul: "The flesh and blood of God is my sole life. I shall perish without it."[270] Even though he was a "great sinner" plagued with a "multitude of infirmities and miseries," Newman realized that he was privileged beyond all words to receive the Lord of Lords in the Eucharist.[271] "I kneel before that Sacred Humanity!" The Eucharist is the sacred Flesh of the Lord conceived in Our Blessed Mother's womb, the very Flesh which suffered crucifixion, and which is now glorified in Heaven. "I adore Thee, O my Saviour, present here as God and man, in soul and body, in true flesh and blood!"[272]

Newman was drawn especially to the source of the Eucharist, the tremendous gift of the Mass, in which the Lord offers Himself as "a daily sacrifice, to the end of time." Through infinite love for us, the Lord has chosen to perpetuate His sacrifice of love on the Cross so that *we* may be as personally present at His saving death as His disciples were at Calvary. "Not simply once, but *every single day*, at every corner of the earth, until the end of time," the Lord Himself, through the ministry of His bishops and priests, continues to offer Himself to His Father! We can hear the Lord Himself saying to us: "My priests shall stand at the Altar, but not they ... *I myself* will be present upon the Altar instead, and *I* will offer up myself invisibly, while they perform the outward rite."[273]

---

[270] St. John Henry Newman, "The Food of the Soul," in *Meditations and Devotions*, 3:15; p. 410.

[271] St. John Henry Newman, "Holy Communion," in *Meditations and Devotions*, 3:15; p. 408.

[272] St. John Henry Newman, "A Short Visit to the Blessed Sacrament before Meditation," in *Meditations and Devotions*, 3; p. 293.

[273] St. John Henry Newman, "Twelve Meditations and Intercessions for Good Friday, 12: Jesus our Daily Sacrifice," in *Meditations and Devotions*, 2:12; p. 203.

The Holy Spirit had shown Newman that the Lord's sacrifice of love for us on the Cross is so tremendous that it must never be forgotten. It must *never* be "an event that is 'done and over.'" No, the Lord's saving death for the world's salvation "*must* remain *present*, though past." And so, in every Mass, the Lord Jesus, who loves us so passionately, has chosen to make present, at every moment and at every place on earth, His one infinite sacrifice of love on the Cross. How magnificent, how "touching and joyful" is this sacred truth! How tremendous is the "infinite compassionateness" of the Lord, who continues to humble Himself in this way, for our sake, until the end of time![274]

Newman longed to make reparation for the unbelief and insults hurled against the Lord, who gives Himself so completely to us in the Sacrament of Love. At Mass, the Lord offers Himself to His Father and gives His own precious Body and Blood to us in the Eucharist. And "the world not only disbelieves, but mocks at this gracious truth." Newman begged the Lord to accept his own worship and adoration in place of the blasphemies of others. "The more men scoff, the more will I believe in Thee ... the hidden Lord of life, who hast done me nothing else but good."[275]

The Church at Worship

As an Anglican priest, Newman fostered practices that manifest a kinship with the Catholic Faith. He had an especially keen sense that the universal Church is in a profound way present whenever people gather to worship as a local community. Newman notes

---

[274] St. John Henry Newman, "The Holy Sacrifice," in *Meditations and Devotions*, 3:15; p. 406.

[275] St. John Henry Newman, "God with us: Jesus the Hidden God," in *Meditations and Devotions*, 3:7.2; pp. 362, 363.

how the first Christians were the Church community "in continual prayer." "They persevered daily with one mind in the Temple, and, breaking bread from house to house," they shared their food "with gladness and singleness of heart, praising God" (see Acts 2:46, 47). Newman was convinced that St. Paul in his epistles "binds" the example of the early Church's "*continual* prayer" on all of us throughout the ages.[276]

Faithful prayer *together* is not only our duty as members of the Church; it is our sacred *privilege*. Newman reminds us what immense "mercy" it is to be able to come to church, to the great "Mercy seat," "to be *permitted* to come" and permitted to come *often*.[277] Convinced of this truth, Newman, as an Anglican priest, initiated the practice of daily services at St. Mary's, even though this was not a custom of the Church of England. [278] Precisely because he did not want to deprive his congregation of so great a "privilege," Newman decided that he would not worry about numbers or be concerned about appearances if only a few people attended the daily services. He recalls the Lord's own assurance that when even "two or three" are gathered in His name, He is in the midst of them (Matt. 18:20). It is true that the Lord's "complete flock" includes everyone, "the old, and the sick, and the infirm, and little children." But even a very small number gathered together in His name is always a "type of His true Church."[279] Such a gathering is a "dwelling-place of the Spirit" and very "precious" to the Lord. And when this small number comes to church, the service itself

---

[276] St. John Henry Newman, "The Daily Service," in *Parochial and Plain Sermons*, Vol. 3, Sermon 21 (London and New York: Longmans, Green, and Co., 1907), p. 301.

[277] Ibid., p. 305.

[278] Ibid., p. 310.

[279] Ibid., pp. 315, 314.

includes, in a profound way, *all* those who cannot come but who are aware of the service and join the congregation in spirit. Even when the number of people gathered is small, "we have with us the *hearts* of many."[280]

When he was serving as an Anglican priest, Newman was convinced that the very existence of daily "services" is a great comfort also to those unable to be there, for through their faith and prayers, they unite themselves to those gathered in church before the "Mercy seat." Together, those who are there, and those who are not able to be there, are sprinkled with the Lord's Blood. They offer themselves with the Lord as a sacrifice of love to the Father and plead for the mercy of the Lord's Blood upon all, especially those struggling with sin. "Who, then, will dare speak of loneliness and solitude" at a service when only a few are gathered? When we gather in church to pray, the angels, too, are with us, guarding us, helping us in our need, and joining us in our worship.[281]

Recognizing the Lord's Presence with Us

As an Anglican priest, Newman grew to realize that this profound understanding of what takes place when we are gathered together in church is not an awareness that we always reach quickly. At first, the disciples themselves did not understand everything that the Lord told them. After He was glorified, however, they were filled with the Holy Spirit at Pentecost, and *then* they understood. The disciples' growth in understanding mirrors our own experience. So often, we do not realize immediately the profound meaning of events in our lives, the good as well as the painful. It is not always easy for us to see that the *Lord* is at work in and among

[280] Ibid., p. 315.
[281] Ibid., p. 316.

us in everything that is permitted to happen to us.[282] Indeed, it is often only afterward that we understand how deeply the Lord Himself was with us.[283]

This may be true especially of the times we have faithfully gone to church in the past. Perhaps we have not truly appreciated the "fragrance" of all these sacred times, the heavenly "pleasure" of being in the Lord's presence. As we grow older, however, the "sweetness" of our past times in church may become clearer to us,[284] and we may begin to see how deeply the Lord was and is *with* us. We may even be filled with "tender, affectionate" thoughts toward those times but not really understand *why*. It is the *sweetness* of the Lord's presence, Newman explains, that we often did not recognize when we were in church. But now, perhaps, the Holy Spirit is opening our eyes to recognize that sweetness. As the years pass, and, with the Lord's grace, when we look back at our past, we may begin to realize what our *deepest* longing truly is: a longing for what only God can give us. It is a longing for *God*.[285]

Newman points especially to memories of receiving Holy Communion perhaps when we were younger, memories that only now may fill us with sweetness. At the time, we may have been bored and could hardly wait until we could leave the church. But now, as we recall the past, we begin to realize that our time in church was not at all boring. In fact, it was "full of God."[286]

It is true that, when we look back on our lives, so many days may seem to have been very ordinary, containing "nothing of Heaven."

---

[282] St. John Henry Newman, "Christ Manifested in Remembrance," in *Parochial and Plain Sermons*, vol. 4, Sermon 17, pp. 255–258.

[283] Ibid., p. 261.

[284] Ibid.

[285] Ibid., p. 262.

[286] Ibid., p. 264.

And yet, Newman assures us, the intimate presence of the Lord Jesus was and is with us, here among us, even more tremendous, more wonderful, than when He walked our earth. Newman urges us to treasure this precious truth and to keep it always in mind.[287] Even when we are not aware of the Lord's presence with us at this particular moment, may we, like the disciples, begin to recognize that the Lord *has* been and *is* with us, especially "in the breaking of the bread." And He *stays* with us. As the Holy Spirit enlightens us about this wonderful truth, may our own hearts, like the hearts of the disciples on the road to Emmaus, "burn" within us (Luke 24:35, 32).[288]

Newman's Anglican Beliefs about Holy Communion

"I am the living bread that came down from heaven. Whoever eats of this bread will live forever; and the bread that I will give for the life of the world is my flesh" (John 6:51).[289] As an Anglican priest, Newman believed that these sacred words of the Lord refer to the "consecrated Bread and Wine of Holy Communion" and that the Anglican church has "never thought *little*" of so great a gift. But he remarks that the faith of Catholics, who believe "even more" about Holy Communion than he himself did as an Anglican, "shows how *great* the gift" truly is. Newman notes that Anglicans do not believe the doctrine of transubstantiation, that the "bread and wine cease to be, and that Christ's sacred Body and Blood are directly seen, touched, and handled, under the appearances of Bread and Wine." As an Anglican priest, Newman believed that

[287] Ibid., p. 265.

[288] St. John Henry Newman, "The Spiritual Presence of Christ in the Church," *Parochial and Plain Sermons*, vol. 6, Sermon 10, p. 134.

[289] St. John Henry Newman, "The Eucharistic Presence," *Parochial and Plain Sermons*, vol. 6, Sermon 11, p. 140.

this Catholic doctrine is an unneeded and unfounded explanation of the Lord's words in Scripture, words that are wonderful enough in themselves.[290]

On the other hand, the Lord Himself has assured us: "Unless you eat the flesh of the Son of Man and drink his blood, you have no life in you" (John 6:53). Newman realized that these sacred words of the Lord declare "a *very great mystery*." Could we possibly think that the Lord, who is truth itself (John 14:6), would use such clear and plain words to promise us a *great gift*, only to deceive and disappoint us? When we hear these words of the Lord to us, will we, too, walk away, like those who took offense at the Lord's words? Or will we, like St. Peter, *welcome* and rejoice in the great gift the Lord offers us? (John 6:66–69).[291]

Newman reflects on those who interpret the Lord's words in John 6 to mean far *less* than the words themselves proclaim. "How can Christ's giving us His Body and Blood mean *merely* His giving us a pledge of His favour?" Newman asks. "Surely these awful words are far too clear and precise to be thus carelessly treated!"[292] As we have noted, Newman the Anglican priest did not believe in the reality of transubstantiation, the Lord's completely changing the substance of the bread and wine into His own precious Body and Blood. And yet, although he did not yet accept the *word transubstantiation*, he was drawing close in belief to what the word *means*. This is why he urges us to pray for the grace truly to appreciate, to long and thirst for, the Lord's presence in the Eucharist and to find our heart's joy in so intimately receiving Him "under the veil of sensible things."[293]

---

[290] Ibid., p. 141.
[291] Ibid., p. 142.
[292] Ibid., p. 143.
[293] Ibid., p. 151.

The Lord has given us every good gift, but the most precious of all is His sacred Body and Blood. What more could He possibly have done for us? And yet we refuse to come to Him that we might have life (John 5:40).[294] Newman stresses that coming to the Lord for life is a "literal bodily action." It is not simply that we come to Him by merely *thinking* about Him. No, "coming to Him" requires *physical* actions from us: our actual *coming* to church and *receiving* Him in Holy Communion. "What is the good of sitting at home seeking Him, when *His Presence* is in the holy Eucharist?"[295]

These are the words of the Lord Himself: "This *is* my body.... This *is* my blood" (Matt. 26:26, 28). "If we refuse to eat that Bread, and drink that Cup," Newman assures us, we are refusing to come to Him that we may have life.[296] He urges us to pray for the grace to have a greater love for and gratitude to the Lord for the tremendous gift of Holy Communion, the sacred foretaste of Heaven. Newman also encourages us to pray for the grace of deepened devotion after we have received the Lord, asking Him to be the healing medicine for our bodies as well as our souls.[297]

The Sacrament of the Eucharist

As we have seen, as an Anglican priest, Newman believed that the Lord is present in the Anglican service of Holy Communion, but he began to realize that, as an Anglican, he could not find all that the Lord had to give him. In the Catholic Church, he found the *realities* that he had longed for as an Anglican: the Sacrifice of the Mass and the Sacrament of the Eucharist. After Newman became

[294] St. John Henry Newman, "Attendance on Holy Communion," in *Parochial and Plain Sermons*, vol. 7, Sermon 11, p. 148.
[295] Ibid., p. 149.
[296] Ibid., p. 150.
[297] Ibid., pp. 156, 157.

a Catholic priest, he fervently preached the *fullness* of the truth that the Eucharist truly is the precious Body and Blood of Jesus.

Newman responds to those who think that Catholics read far more into these words of the Lord than He intended: "Unless you eat the flesh of the Son of Man and drink his blood, you have no life in you" (John 6:53). Newman stresses this profound truth: "Either *no* gift is given in the Eucharist," or else a gift is given to us "beyond words." *There is no alternative.* The Lord Himself says, "Take, eat, this is *my body*" (Matt. 26:26). The Lord either *means* what His words say, or His words mean *nothing*.[298]

When he began preaching as a Catholic priest in the church of the Catholic University of Ireland, Newman spoke with even deeper affection and tenderness about the "intimate, immediate" knowledge of the Lord, which is "the ordinary feeling" and response of fervent Catholics, especially after receiving the Lord in Holy Communion. An acquaintance of Newman's who was not Catholic had read a book by a Catholic author who wrote as if he had a deeply "personal attachment" to the Lord. "It was as if he had *seen* Him, *known* Him, *lived with* Him."[299]

Newman remarks that this is the very same impression that often strikes others who are not Catholic and who come to Mass. They often notice that Catholics seem to attend Mass not out of a sense of duty but rather because they love the Lord and have a true "*familiarity*" with Him. How else can we explain the "spontaneous postures of devotion," the "heedlessness of the presence

---

[298] St. John Henry Newman, "Difficulties in the Scripture Proof of the Catholic Creed," in *Discussions and Arguments on Various Subjects*, 3:1.2 (London: Longmans, Green, 1907), p. 119.

[299] St. John Henry Newman, "Waiting for Christ," in *Sermons Preached on Various Occasions* (London: Longmans, Green, 1908), p. 42.

of others," which Catholics display especially at the Consecration of the Mass?[300]

Those who are not Catholic often are moved by the stillness, the silence, the *worship* of Catholics at Mass, especially at the sacred moment of the Consecration. These visitors feel this profound "effect," Newman notes, but they do not understand its *cause*. Something *tremendous* has happened at Mass, in their very midst: the Lord *Himself* is now *present* on the altar, there to be loved and adored.[301]

Through His ordained bishops and priests, Newman stresses, the Lord continues until the end of time to give Himself completely to us: "This *is* my body.... This *is* my blood" (Matt. 26:26, 28). By the power of his priesthood, every priest, weak and subject to sin, is still the one through whom the Lord makes Himself present upon the altar and gives Himself to us in the Eucharist. And we who receive the Lord, we who also are weak and sinful, receive and welcome the Lord of Lords into our inmost being.[302] When we know the Lord only as the all-powerful God, Newman notes, we know Him only partially. We begin to know the Lord *intimately* when we also know Him in His sacred *humanness*. This is why, through infinite love for us, the Lord of Heaven and earth gives us His precious Body and Blood under the humble appearances of bread and wine. He gives *Himself* to us, even to *eat*.[303]

From his own experience as a Catholic priest, Newman tenderly comments that the mysteries of revelation that Catholics believe, incomprehensible as they are in themselves to our human reason, still "are most gracious, most loving, laden with mercy and consolation

---

[300] Ibid.

[301] Ibid, p. 43.

[302] St. John Henry Newman, "Omnipotence in Bonds," in *Sermons Preached on Various Occasions*, p. 87.

[303] Ibid., p. 88.

to us, not only sublime" but also "touching and winning." In particular, the Catholic belief in the Real Presence of the Lord in the Eucharist surely "is not more mysterious" than the very eternity of the Trinity, who exist without beginning or end. When Catholics hear the truth proclaimed that God the Son has become flesh of our flesh, has been beaten and scourged and nailed to a cross by His creatures for love of us, Catholics are filled with awe and worship before the Lord. So, too, Newman comments, Catholics bow in adoration before the Lord who, in infinite love and humility, chooses to give Himself to us under the species of simple Bread, and to "suffer Himself to be hidden in a small tabernacle."[304]

Again speaking from his own experience, Newman assures us that the Catholic belief in the Lord's true presence in our tabernacles "overpowers our heart; it is the most subduing, affecting, piercing thought which can be pictured to us." This sacred mystery "thrills through us, and draws our tears, and abases us, and melts us into love and affection!" The most tender, most compassionate Lord of Lords does not want to frighten us by His power but rather to attract us by His tenderness. He wishes us to know His "infinite bountifulness" but also His humble "condescension" and infinite compassion for us in our weakness.[305]

Newman invites us to gaze on the splendors of creation in order to glimpse the "unimaginable glory" of the Lord, whose *most* wondrous gift is *Himself* in the Eucharist. Let us look upon the mountains and the sea and "drink in the fragrant air" of spring. Let us walk in a beautiful garden and be delighted with the grace,

---

[304] St. John Henry Newman, "Mysteries of Nature and of Grace," in *Discourses to Mixed Congregations* (London: Longmans, Green, 1906), pp. 267–268.

[305] Ibid., p. 268.

beauty, and sweetness of the myriads of kinds of flowers. These wonders are but "the poorest and dimmest glimmerings" of the *Lord's* own infinite beauty. Compared with His beautiful creation, the Lord Himself, in all His glory, *infinitely* exceeds "all that is graceful, gentle, sweet, and fair on earth." "Say not" that the Lord *Himself* is "not enough" for us, not enough to fill and satiate us completely with beauty, love, and joy![306]

As a Catholic priest, Newman fell in love especially with the feast of Corpus Christi, the feast of the Lord's precious Body and Blood. "There is no feast which shows more wonderfully what Christianity is!" Newman loved this feast because it so publicly and jubilantly honors the Lord in the Eucharist.[307] The miracles that the Lord worked while He walked on earth are full of wonder, Newman comments, but the "great miracle of the Altar" is incomparable. In the Mass, Jesus works today and every day "the *most* wonderful of miracles."[308] The same Lord who performed miracles of healing and who raised people from the dead is in the tabernacle in every Catholic church. He is *physically* close to us and within us, and we can speak to Him as intimately as the disciples did long ago.[309] "Wonderful communion!" Newman cries out.

---

[306] St. John Henry Newman, "The Mystery of Divine Condescension," in *Discourses to Mixed Congregations*, pp. 296, 297.

[307] St. John Henry Newman, "Devotion to the Holy Eucharist," in *Sermon Notes of John Henry Cardinal Newman 1849–1878*, ed. Fathers of the Birmingham Oratory (London: Longmans, Green, 1913), p. 127.

[308] St. John Henry Newman, "The Omnipotence of God the Reason for Faith and Hope," in *Faith and Prejudice and Other Unpublished Sermons*. ed. Birmingham Oratory (New York: Sheed and Ward, 1956), pp. 24, 26.

[309] St. John Henry Newman, "Devotion to the Holy Eucharist," 4; p. 129.

The Wonders of the Mass and the Eucharist

The Lord's tender presence to us at Mass and in the Eucharist is our joy, our delight, our very life![310]

Newman reminds us that the Lord Jesus, our great High Priest, unceasingly offers up the sacrifice of Himself to His Father in Heaven. This "*heavenly* Mass" offered by the Lord never ceases, and "the *Mass* is but the *earthly* presence of it." While the Lord offers Himself to the Father both in Heaven and on earth, the entire Church is joined to Him in intercession: our Blessed Mother and all the angels and saints in Heaven and all of us here on earth. Indeed, all intercessory prayer has power ultimately through the Mass.[311]

Newman urges us to attend daily Mass as often as we can and to spend time just being with the Lord in the Blessed Sacrament. In this way, our intentions and prayers, especially for our loved ones, will be received into the very heart of the Lord, and our own hearts will be filled with deepening love for Him. *This* is how the saints have become saints, Newman assures us. "They were not saints all at once, but by little and little. And so we, who are not saints, must still proceed *by the same road*," drawing all our love, joy, and strength from the Lord in the Eucharist.[312]

May the beautiful insights and intercession of St. John Henry Newman help us to grow in our love for the Mass and the Lord in the Eucharist and encourage us to proceed to our heavenly home by the same wonderful road by which every saint has traveled.

---

[310] Ibid., 5, 6; p. 129.

[311] St. John Henry Newman, "The Mass," in *Sermon Notes*, pp. 193, 194.

[312] St. John Henry Newman, "The Calls of Grace," in *Faith and Prejudice and Other Sermons*, pp. 50–51.

6

St. Thérèse of Lisieux and St. John Vianney

The Gift of Frequent Holy Communion

In 1873, when St. John Henry Newman was in his seventies, St. Thérèse of Lisieux was born. Her birth also was almost fifteen years after the death of St. John Vianney, the "Curé d'Ars." Both Thérèse and Vianney lived in France, leading humble lives marked by a profound love for the Eucharist and a zeal to draw others to this wondrous Sacrament of the Lord's love for us.

St. Thérèse of Lisieux

St. Thérèse of the Child Jesus and the Holy Face (1873–1897) died at the age of twenty-four after a brief hidden life in the Carmel of Lisieux, France. Today, countless people know and love her and are inspired to live her "Little Way" of love and trust. But we owe much more to St. Thérèse than we may realize. It was her longing for daily Holy Communion and later her intercession for it that provided compelling support for Pope St. Pius X's decrees encouraging daily reception of Holy Communion and enabling children to receive Holy Communion at an earlier age.[313]

---

[313] Pope Pius X's 1905 decree *Sacra Tridentina* encouraged frequent Communion, and his 1910 decree *Quam Singulari* permitted

The Wonders of the Mass and the Eucharist

Louis Martin and Marie-Azélie "Zélie" Guérin, now canonized saints, were blessed with nine children, the youngest of whom was Thérèse. Their five daughters who lived to adulthood all became nuns, four of them entering the Carmel at Lisieux. Only four years old when her mother died, Thérèse was lovingly cared for by her beloved Papa, her two oldest sisters, Marie and Pauline, and her mother's family, the Guérins. When both Pauline and Marie eventually entered the Carmelite monastery of Lisieux, Thérèse attended school at the Benedictine convent of Notre-Dame-du-Prè as a day student. It was there that, on May 8, 1884, at the age of eleven, she received her First Holy Communion.

When Thérèse was thirteen, she left the Benedictine school and continued her education through private lessons at home. Inspired by her burning love for Jesus and the example of her sisters, Thérèse longed to enter the Carmelite monastery. When she was only fourteen, she begged this favor of Pope Leo XIII during a pilgrimage to Rome with her father and her older sister Céline. Thérèse did receive permission to join Carmel in 1888, when she was fifteen years old. As a Carmelite nun, Thérèse lived a humble life of hidden holiness, practicing her Little Way of "spiritual childhood," doing everything with love, trust, and surrender to the Lord.

In 1893, when she was only twenty, Thérèse was appointed to serve as assistant novice mistress. The following year, her beloved Papa died, having endured heartbreaking physical and mental sufferings following a stroke. After his death, Céline, who had been caring for him, joined her three sisters at Carmel. Her cousin Marie Guérin, to whom Thérèse also was very close, entered the same

---

children who have reached the age of reason to receive Holy Communion. In both decrees, the pope made clear that he was not instituting new practices but rather restoring ancient ones.

Carmel. In the Lisieux Carmel, therefore, Thérèse was surrounded by loved family members. When she was only twenty-three years old, the prioress, Mother Agnes (Thérèse's sister Pauline), asked Thérèse to write down memories of her childhood and family life for the benefit only of her family. Thus began Thérèse's work on her treasured autobiography, *L'Histoire d'une âme*, *The Story of a Soul*. That very same year, early on Good Friday of 1896, Thérèse coughed up blood for the first time, signaling the tuberculosis from which she would die. As she endured intense physical and spiritual sufferings, Thérèse wrote letters to her family and friends and continued to counsel the novices. During the last year of Thérèse's life, the prioress, the very difficult Mother Marie de Gonzague, told her to continue writing her *Story of a Soul* by including memories of her nine years at Carmel. After months of excruciating suffering caused by the tuberculosis, Thérèse died on September 30, 1897.

At Carmel, Thérèse had lived her Little Way of holiness, doing everything, small as it might be, with love and complete trust in the Lord. She had never intended her *Story of a Soul* to be seen by anyone except family members. As she neared her death, however, the Holy Spirit inspired her to believe that many others could profit from learning about her Little Way of holiness. Through the efforts of her beloved sister and "second mother," Mother Agnes, who had served as prioress at the Lisieux Carmel from 1893 to 1896, Thérèse's *Story of a Soul* was published the year after her death, though in a very much edited version. Nevertheless, Thérèse's profound insights, written with simplicity and deep affection and illumining the path of love available to everyone in every walk of life, touched the hearts of countless readers.

Mother Agnes sent the manuscript of Thérèse's *Story of a Soul* to diocesan and then Vatican officials. Deeply moved and inspired by Thérèse's manuscript, diocesan officials began in 1910 the process inquiring into Thérèse's holiness. In 1914, before his death that year, Pope Pius X opened the apostolic process for Thérèse's canonization. Pope Pius XI canonized her in 1925, and a century after her death, St. John Paul II named Thérèse the third of four women Doctors of the Church.

Thérèse's Longing for Daily Holy Communion

Even when she was a small child, the Holy Spirit filled Thérèse with a great longing to attend Mass and to receive the Lord in Holy Communion. To receive Jesus was her entire "joy and desire."[314] When Pauline was preparing Thérèse's older sister Céline for her First Communion, Thérèse, only seven at the time, begged to attend the lessons. The customary age for First Holy Communion was eleven, but Thérèse considered this *far* too long to wait.[315] When Céline received her First Holy Communion, Thérèse was so touched that she later remembered the day as one of the "most beautiful" of her life.[316]

Several years later, as Thérèse neared the age at which she could receive the Lord, she was disappointed to learn that her birthday on January 2 prevented her from joining the class at her school preparing for Holy Communion. Her birthday was only one day later than the January 1 deadline, and she absolutely could not understand such a "severe rule" that required her to wait an *entire year* to receive the Lord. When Thérèse saw the bishop of Lisieux

---

[314] Mother Agnes, in *Witnesses of the Apostolic Canonization Process of Thérèse of Lisieux, 1915–1916*, Witness Six, 374, 379. Archives du Carmel de Lisieux.

[315] Sr. Geneviève of St. Teresa (Céline), in *Witnesses of the Apostolic Canonization Process*, Witness Eight, 662.

[316] St. Thérèse of Lisieux, *Story of a Soul*, trans. John Clarke, O.C.D. (Washington, D.C.: ICS Publications, 1976), p. 57.

walking in town one day, she longed to stop him and ask his permission to receive her First Communion without waiting until she was eleven. When her oldest sister, Marie, told her that among the early Christians, even little children received the Holy Eucharist, Thérèse demanded, "Why is it not like that *now*?"[317]

When the time finally came for Thérèse to prepare for her First Communion, she wrote to her sister Pauline, who was now in Carmel. Known as Sr. Agnes of Jesus, Pauline had sent Thérèse a small prayer book to use as she prepared to receive the Lord. Thérèse wrote to Pauline that one of the prayers in the book Pauline had sent her had very much inspired her, and she longed to make her heart a beautiful garden for the Lord. Thérèse wanted the Lord to be so pleased to dwell within her that He would not even *think* of "going back to heaven."[318] She delighted in offering daily acts of love and sacrifice to the Lord and writing them down in a notebook that Pauline had given her.[319]

Thérèse finally was blessed to receive her First Holy Communion at the Benedictine Abbey of Lisieux on May 8, 1884, when she was eleven years old. This wondrous day remained "engraved" in her heart. She treasured every detail of that "*heavenly* day": the loving affection of the teachers and the older students; the girls in their beautiful white dresses; the solemn procession into the chapel; the exquisite music. But the *deepest* graces of that day she

---

[317] Sr. Marie of the Sacred Heart, (Marie), in *Witnesses of the Apostolic Canonization Process*, Witness Seven, 565.

[318] St. Thérèse, Letter 11, to Sr. Mary Agnes, March 1884; in *St. Thérèse of Lisieux General Correspondence*, vol. 1, trans. John Clarke, O.C.D. (Washington, D.C., Institute of Carmelite Studies, 1982), p. 191.

[319] Mother Agnes, in *Witnesses of the Apostolic Canonization Process*, Witness Six, 421.

could not describe. "There are deep *spiritual thoughts* which cannot be expressed in human language without losing their intimate and heavenly meaning."[320]

Soon after receiving the Lord for the first time, Thérèse wrote, "How sweet was that first kiss of Jesus.... It was a kiss of *love*; I felt that I was *loved*, and I said: 'I love You, and I give myself to You forever.'" Before her First Holy Communion, Thérèse tells us, she and the Lord Jesus would spend time simply looking at each other with love. But when she received the Lord within her for the first time, the union was so profound that "Jesus alone remained." Overcome with joy, she could only let the tears run down her face. The other girls thought that Thérèse was sad because she missed her mother, who had died, or that she was longing for the presence of her sister Pauline. Thérèse's companions saw her tears but did not understand their cause. "*All the joy of Heaven*" had entered her soul. Completely overwhelmed, Thérèse could only weep for joy.[321]

Indeed, how could she weep from *sorrow*, when "Heaven itself" was in her soul? And because she trusted that her beloved Mamma had long ago taken her place in Heaven, Thérèse was certain that her mother was intimately with her as she received the Lord. In "receiving Jesus' visit," she writes, "I received also Mamma's. She blessed me and rejoiced at my happiness." How beautiful is Thérèse's insight! When we receive the Lord in Holy Communion, in some profound way, our loved ones in Heaven are also with us, for *Heaven* itself is in our souls. Thérèse also was deeply touched that she was chosen to make the Act of Consecration to Our Blessed Mother in the name of all the girls, especially since her own mother had died when she was so young. "I put all

[320] St. Thérèse, *Story of a Soul*, pp. 73, 77.
[321] Ibid., p. 77.

my heart into speaking to her." On that day, Thérèse consecrated herself to our Blessed Mother as her own child, begging her to keep watch over her. And then Thérèse savored the delight of being with her family for the celebration that evening.[322]

Although the joy of her First Holy Communion stayed deep in her heart the day afterward, Thérèse felt a certain sadness. She loved the exquisite Communion dress her oldest sister, Marie, had bought her, and she enjoyed with gratitude the wonderful gifts that her family had lavished on her. But only Jesus could truly satisfy her heart, and all that she could think about was when she could receive the Lord again. About a month after her First Communion, Thérèse went to Confession and got up the courage to ask the priest if she could receive Holy Communion a *second* time. "Against all hope," the priest said yes. Thérèse then had the immense joy of kneeling at the Communion rail with her Papa and her beloved sister Marie. "What a sweet memory I have of this second visit of Jesus! My tears flowed again with an ineffable sweetness." Thérèse kept repeating to herself, "It is no longer I that live; it is Jesus who lives in me!" (Gal. 2:20).[323]

Thérèse continued to attend school at the Benedictine abbey, but she didn't have anyone with whom she was particularly close. Often, she tells us, she felt "very much alone." This trial served only to deepen her love for and devotion to the Lord in the Blessed Sacrament. Her one consolation at school became the time she habitually spent in prayer before the Blessed Sacrament as she waited for her father to pick her up. The Lord Jesus was her "*only Friend.*"[324]

---

[322] Ibid., p. 78.
[323] Ibid., p. 79.
[324] Ibid., p. 87.

The Wonders of the Mass and the Eucharist

At the age of thirteen, Thérèse stopped attending the Abbey school, but her confessor permitted her to receive Holy Communion four or five times a week, more often than she had thought possible. Later, when she was a professed nun at Carmel, Thérèse wrote of how much her audacity had grown since that time. For as long as she could remember, she had been consumed with the longing to receive the Lord *every day*. But rather than telling her confessor about her longing, she had simply followed her confessor's instructions about how often she could receive the Lord. With time, however, Thérèse grew to regret not having acted with more "*boldness*" in making known to her confessor her vehement desire for *daily* Holy Communion![325]

Thérèse tells us of the time when she was fourteen and her father took Céline and her on a pilgrimage to Paris and Rome. At Paris, what delighted her most was the shrine of Our Lady of Victories. Deeply affected by the death of her mother when she was only four, Thérèse felt the Blessed Virgin smiling upon her and assuring her that she was "*her* child." "I could no longer give her any other name but 'Mamma,' as this appeared ever so much more tender than 'Mother.'" Thérèse was so overcome by the graces she received through our Blessed Mother at her shrine that she wept, just as she had done at her First Communion.[326]

At Carmel: *Thérèse's Longing for Daily Holy Communion*

At the age of fifteen, Thérèse received permission to enter Carmel. She was filled with anticipation at the prospect of being able to receive *daily* Holy Communion. The prioress, Mother Marie de Gonzague, however, was opposed to the practice of daily Communion,

[325] Ibid., p. 104.
[326] Ibid., p. 123.

and, according to custom, it was *she* who determined how often each sister could receive the Lord. Although the entire community suffered from her "passionately jealous nature," Mother Marie de Gonzague was elected prioress several times and served in that position for a total of twenty-one years. She governed by imposing her will on the community. Even more "dreadful," she would decide arbitrarily which sisters would be permitted to receive Holy Communion.[327]

Heartbroken, Thérèse began praying fervently that daily Holy Communion at the monastery would be permitted.[328] Her prayers were answered three years after she entered Carmel. In a decree published in 1891, Pope Leo XIII gave spiritual directors, *not* religious superiors, the authority to determine how often sisters could receive the Lord.[329] Thérèse was overjoyed. Mother Marie de Gonzague at first seemed obedient to the decree. In fact, however, she was angry that this power had been removed from her. She made known her displeasure when the confessor, Fr. Louis-Auguste Youf, allowed several sisters to receive the Lord daily. Fearing her wrath, Fr. Youf was intimidated into allowing the prioress again to decide when the sisters could receive the Lord.[330] For most of the nine and a half years of her religious life, Thérèse was not permitted to receive daily Holy Communion. Unable to receive the Lord as

---

[327] Mother Agnes, in *Witnesses of the Apostolic Canonization Process,* Witness Six, 358, 359, 361.

[328] Ibid., 422.

[329] Pope Leo XIII, decree *Quemadmodum,* December 17, 1890; Mother Agnes, in *Witnesses of the Apostolic Canonization Process,* Witness Six, 361.

[330] Mother Agnes, in *Witnesses of the Apostolic Canonization Process,* Witness Six, 379.

often as she wanted, she would pray to the Lord, "Remain in *me* as in a tabernacle."[331]

This profound insight of Thérèse is also one of her most precious gifts to us. The Lord Himself comes to us in Holy Communion, and yet His intimate sacramental presence is possible only as long as the sacred species lasts, for perhaps fifteen minutes. Every time we receive the Lord in Holy Communion, however, the Lord also deepens His presence within us through sanctifying grace, so that He *remains* in us, through grace, as in His abiding home (John 14:23) and Heaven.

The Holy Spirit taught Thérèse that the Lord's deepest purpose in coming to us in Holy Communion is not only to give us the most precious gift of His sacramental presence but also to live in us through sanctifying grace at every moment and *never* to leave us. This, too, is His beautiful purpose in dwelling in the tabernacle night and day: "It is not to remain in a golden ciborium that He comes to us each day from Heaven." No, Thérèse assures us, "it's to find *another* heaven, infinitely more dear to Him than the first: the *heaven of our soul* ... the living temple of the adorable Trinity."[332]

Because it is such a profound privilege for us to receive the precious Body and Blood of the Lord in the Eucharist, Thérèse also understood how important it is that we acknowledge our sins at the beginning of Mass. As we prepare our hearts to receive the Lord, let us cry out to the Lord with the publican, "Be merciful to me, a sinner" (Luke 18:13). Thérèse recounts how she herself once was overwhelmed by tears of contrition as she prepared her heart at the beginning of Mass. "How impossible

[331] St. Thérèse, *Story of a Soul*, p. 276.
[332] Ibid., p. 104.

it is to give oneself such sentiments! It is the *Holy Spirit* who inspires them."[333]

In one brief but precious period, during her nine and a half years at Carmel, Thérèse *was* blessed to receive the Lord every day. Almost all the sisters in the monastery had become seriously ill with a deadly case of the flu. Only Thérèse and two other sisters were not bedridden. Those who were most ill were cared for by sisters who themselves were extremely weak. As the assistant sacristan, Thérèse had to assume all the responsibilities of the sacristan, who had become seriously ill. Thérèse's nineteenth birthday was marked by the death of one of the sisters, and soon afterward, two more sisters in the monastery died. It was Thérèse who had to prepare for all three burials. All through these severe trials, Thérèse writes, the Lord granted her the deepest desires of her heart. "I had the unspeakable consolation of receiving Holy Communion *every day.* Ah! this was sweet indeed! Jesus spoiled me." "He permitted me *to receive Him* while the rest didn't have this same happiness."[334]

Thérèse loved serving as assistant sacristan, a responsibility that she considered to be "worthy of angels."[335] She often repeated these beautiful words of Scripture in her heart: "You are to be holy, you who carry the vessels of the Lord" (see Isa. 52:11). The grace of being permitted to touch and handle the sacred vessels and linens for Mass filled her with joy.[336] Thérèse felt tremendously blessed to share "with priests" the privilege of touching the sacred vessels, the large host, and the linens used for Mass, and she would kiss

---

[333] Mother Agnes, in *Witnesses of the Apostolic Canonization Process,* Witness Six, 485-486.

[334] St. Thérèse, *Story of a Soul,* pp. 171, 172.

[335] Sr. Thérèse of St. Augustine, in *Witnesses of the Apostolic Canonization Process,* Witness Nine, 816.

[336] St. Thérèse, *Story of a Soul,* p. 172.

them with great love and devotion.[337] She also told her sister Céline about the grace-filled time that the sacred Host had fallen out of the chaplain's hands at Holy Communion time. When Thérèse received the sacred Host in her scapular, she felt blessed, as our Mother Mary was, to hold the Lord Jesus close to her.[338]

And yet, Thérèse confesses, *feelings* of devotion after she received Holy Communion were rare for her. "I can't say that I frequently received consolations when making my thanksgivings after Mass; perhaps it is the time I receive the least." She would ask our Blessed Mother and the saints and angels to welcome the Lord for her. Even as she suffered from "distractions and sleepiness" after receiving the Lord, she resolved to be especially grateful during the rest of the day. In this way, she felt that she was pleasing the Lord by finding a way to "profit" from her "miseries."[339] "Really, I am far from being a saint," Thérèse writes, admitting that she *should* have felt "desolate" because of the countless times she fell asleep after receiving the Lord in Holy Communion. But she did not. On the contrary, she was consoled to remember that "*little children are as pleasing to their parents when they are asleep as when they are wide awake.*"[340]

Thérèse's Longing for Holy Communion during Her Last Illness

In early 1896, when she was twenty-three, Thérèse began to suffer from a chronic sore throat and coughing. On the night between Holy Thursday and Good Friday, April 2–3, 1896, she coughed

[337] Sr. Marie of the Trinity, in *Witnesses of the Apostolic Canonization Process*, Witness Twenty-One, 1227.

[338] Sr. Geneviève of St. Teresa (Céline), in *Witnesses of the Apostolic Canonization Process*, Witness Eight, 662.

[339] St. Thérèse, *Story of a Soul*, pp. 172, 173.

[340] Ibid., p. 165.

up blood. During the months that followed, she began to suffer more and more acutely, but she never lost her ardent desire to receive the Lord in Holy Communion. After suffering all night from pain, cold, and sleeplessness, she would try to make her way to the chapel for Mass and Holy Communion.[341]

One morning, after seeing Thérèse struggle back to her cell, Mother Agnes followed her, only to hear Thérèse tell her, "This is not suffering too much to gain one Communion."[342] Nevertheless, Thérèse did not want Mother Agnes to be distressed even if Thérèse happened to die without being able to receive the Lord: "It's a great grace to receive the sacraments; but when God doesn't allow it, it's good just the same. Everything is a grace."[343]

Two and a half months before her death, one of the sisters suggested that Thérèse might be privileged to die after she had received the Lord on the feast of Our Lady of Mount Carmel. Thérèse was convinced that this would not happen: it "would be too fine a death for me." "Everything I do, little souls must be able to do, too."[344] And yet, despite her increasing struggles, Thérèse still longed to be able to receive Jesus daily if she could, a privilege still not customary at the monastery. "They don't believe I'm as sick as I am. So it makes it all the harder to be deprived of Holy Communion."[345] As swallowing became more and more difficult for her, Thérèse would thank Mother Agnes for asking that she be

---

[341] Sr. Thérèse of St. Augustine, in *Witnesses of the Apostolic Canonization Process*, Witness Nine, 816.

[342] *St. Thérèse of Lisieux: Her Last Conversations*, trans. John Clarke, O.C.D. (Washington, D.C.: Institute of Carmelite Studies, 1977), p. 255.

[343] Ibid., p. 57.

[344] Mother Agnes, in *Witnesses of the Apostolic Process*, Witness Six, 420.

[345] St. Thérèse, *Her Last Conversations*, p. 63.

given at least a very small particle of the sacred Host, thus allowing her to receive the Lord. On one occasion, she told Mother Agnes, "How happy I was to have God in my heart! I cried as on the day of my First Communion."[346]

As the time passed, Thérèse's sufferings intensified. The nuns' physician had wanted to give her morphine injections to ease her suffering, but Mother Marie de Gonzague would not allow it. Thérèse continued to suffer unbearable pain. One day, she confessed to her sister, Mother Agnes, that, without faith, she would have been driven to despair, and she warned that possible means of suicide should never be left near those suffering so violently.[347] On August 19, 1897, Thérèse told Mother Agnes that she felt like she was losing her "wits." "Last night, I couldn't take it anymore; I begged the Blessed Virgin to hold my head in her hands so that I could take my sufferings."[348]

Because of her violent coughing and vomiting, Thérèse received Holy Communion for the last time on August 19, 1897. This heartache intensified her agonies.[349] Since her childhood, she had longed to receive the Lord every day of her life. Now, as she faced her death, she had to suffer the pain of never again receiving the Lord in the Eucharist. Rather than being the infinite blessing that she had always longed for, receiving Holy Communion had become a torment for Thérèse, increasing her violent coughing, vomiting, and gasping to take the next breath.

---

[346] Ibid., pp. 57–58. About her tears at her First Holy Communion, see *Story of a Soul*, p. 77.

[347] Mother Agnes, in *Witnesses of the Apostolic Canonization Process*, Witness Six, 505, 506.

[348] St. Thérèse, *Her Last Conversations*, p. 154.

[349] Mother Agnes, in *Witnesses of the Apostolic Canonization Process*, Witness Six, 507.

Thérèse dreaded having an accident after receiving the Lord. Instead of making the decision herself, she wanted to be told in *obedience* not to receive the Eucharist. But because she said nothing, the sisters would *insist* that she receive at least a small particle of a sacred Host, believing that they were following her wishes. On August 20, Thérèse could no longer restrain herself. Absolutely unable to receive even a small particle of Holy Communion, she began to choke and sob so violently that Mother Agnes finally realized the deepest source of her agony. It broke her heart to see Thérèse so "close to dying of *sorrow*." Thérèse begged Mother Agnes not even to look at her: "I would cry too much if I were to tell you my troubles right now, and I'm having such difficulty in breathing that I would certainly suffocate." Thérèse never received Holy Communion again.[350]

After weeks of suffering unimaginable pain, Thérèse died on the evening of September 30, 1897. The customary photo taken immediately after death gives evidence of what those present witnessed. Thérèse died with a "sublime expression" on her face that made her "ravishingly beautiful." Her last words were, "My God, I love You."[351]

As we have seen, almost two years before her death, in the winter of 1895, Thérèse had begun to write her *L'Histoire d'une âme*, her *Story of a Soul*. She did this in obedience to her sister, Mother Agnes, who served as prioress from 1894 to 1896. Thérèse's oldest sister, Sr. Marie of the Sacred Heart, is the one who had encouraged Mother Agnes to ask Thérèse to write down her childhood memories, *just* for their family. Thérèse wrote the first eight

[350] Mother Agnes, in *Her Last Conversations*, pp. 157, 158.
[351] Mother Agnes, in *Witnesses of the Apostolic Process*, Witness Six, 509, 510.

chapters of her *Story of a Soul* and gave them to Mother Agnes in January 1896. Then Mother Marie de Gonzague was once again elected prioress.

In June 1897, Mother Agnes convinced Mother Marie de Gonzague to ask Thérèse to continue her story. In obedience, Thérèse complied with the request, writing the second part of *Story of a Soul*, chapters 9 and 10, and addressing them to Mother Marie de Gonzague. At the request of Sr. Marie of the Sacred Heart, Thérèse had written the last chapter on the "Little Way" of love in 1896, during a retreat.[352]

In a telling passage from this last section of her autobiography, Thérèse recounts how she had discovered the mystery of love to which we are all called, the mystery of love for the Lord Jesus and for one another, rooted in the precious Sacrament of the Eucharist. At the Last Supper, when the Lord had given nothing less than Himself "in the unspeakable mystery" of the Eucharist, He spoke to His apostles and to every one of us with "inexpressible tenderness: 'A new commandment I give you, that you love one another: that as *I* have loved you, you also love one another'" (John 13:34).[353]

Advocate and Intercessor for Daily Holy Communion

Before her death, Thérèse had promised that from Heaven she would gain wonderful blessings for the community, graces that would flow down upon them like a "shower of roses." Foremost among this "shower of blessings was undoubtedly the gift of daily Communion," a grace granted to Thérèse's community immediately

---

[352] Mother Agnes, in *Witnesses of the Apostolic Canonization Process*, Witness Six, 500, 501; Sr. Marie of the Sacred Heart, in *Witnesses of the Apostolic Canonization Process*, Witness Seven, 613.

[353] St. Thérèse, *Story of a Soul*, p. 219.

after her death.[354] We recall that, when Thérèse entered Carmel, Mother Marie de Gonzague, who was opposed to daily Holy Communion, was the one who determined when each sister could receive the Lord. When Thérèse realized this, she began to pray ardently that the pope would issue a decree freeing monasteries from the rules and customs that prevented daily Communion.[355]

She particularly prayed to St. Joseph for this intention. As we have seen, in 1891, Pope Leo XIII did issue a decree stating that it would no longer be religious superiors but rather confessors who could permit sisters to receive daily Holy Communion. Thérèse was certain that this blessing was due to St. Joseph's intercession.[356] Nevertheless, Mother Marie de Gonzague continued her opposition to allowing the sisters to receive Holy Communion daily. Before Thérèse died, however, she promised Mother Marie de Gonzague that, from *Heaven*, she would make her change her mind. A week after Thérèse's death, Fr. Youf died, and Fr. Hodierne became chaplain. He made it his practice to give the sisters Holy Communion *every* day. Wondrously, rather than objecting, Mother Marie de Gonzague seemed to be pleased.[357]

Another incident in Thérèse's life later provided Pope St. Pius X with precious support for the decree that he published in 1905, encouraging the practice of frequent Holy Communion. When

[354] Sr. Thérèse of St. Augustine, in *Witnesses of the Apostolic Canonization Process*, Witness Nine, 817.

[355] Mother Agnes, in *Witnesses of the Apostolic Canonization Process*, Witness Six, 422.

[356] Sr. Geneviève of St. Teresa (Céline), in *Witnesses of the Apostolic Canonization Process*, Witness Eight, 668.

[357] Sr. Marie of the Sacred Heart, in *Witnesses of the Ordinary Canonization Process*, Witness Three, 314, Archives du Carmel de Lisieux; Mother Agnes, in *Witnesses of the Apostolic Canonization Process*, Witness Six, 495.

The Wonders of the Mass and the Eucharist

Thérèse had been only a sixteen-year-old novice, her beloved nineteen-year-old cousin Marie Guérin (later Sr. Marie of the Eucharist of the Lisieux Carmel), wrote to Thérèse begging her counsel. Suffering from scruples, Marie was troubled by her reaction to statues she viewed in the Paris Exposition. Afraid of committing sacrilege, she had decided to refrain from receiving the Lord in Holy Communion.

On May 30, 1889, the sixteen-year-old Thérèse wrote to Marie this extraordinary response: "You haven't committed the shadow of any evil; I know what these kinds of temptations are so well that I can assure you of this without any fear." "Besides, Jesus tells me this in the depths of my heart." It is not sin that Marie has committed, Thérèse assures her. What has been plaguing Marie are not sins but temptations. "We must *despise* all these temptations and pay *no* attention whatsoever to them."[358]

Thérèse confessed that she *was* grieved, not by the temptations Marie was suffering but by the fact that Marie had stopped receiving the Lord in Holy Communion. The devil tries to make us believe that temptations are sins, in this way robbing us of our peace and "depriving Jesus of a loved tabernacle." Failing to lure those who love Jesus into serious sin, the devil draws them instead to deprive themselves of Holy Communion. In this way, the devil wins, and "Jesus weeps."[359]

"Oh, my darling," Thérèse writes, the Lord "is burning with the desire to enter your heart." "Don't listen to the devil." "Go without any fear to receive Jesus in peace and love." Thérèse writes that she understands from experience what it is to suffer from scrupulosity.

[358] St. Thérèse, Letter 92, to Marie Guérin, May 30, 1889; in *St. Thérèse of Lisieux, General Correspondence*, vol. 1, p. 567.
[359] Ibid.

She knows well the devil's wiles in trying to make us think that we commit sacrilege by receiving the Lord when we are suffering temptations. But this is not true. "Go without any fear to receive your only true Friend." Writing in the third person, Thérèse notes that the Lord had given her the grace to receive Him, "even when she believed that she had committed great sins." Receiving the Lord in Holy Communion was "the sole means of *ridding* herself" of the devil's attacks. What offends the Lord is not the temptations we suffer, Thérèse assures her cousin. "What offends Him and what wounds His Heart is the lack of confidence!" Knowing that we have only a limited time here on earth to love Jesus, the devil tries in every way possible to keep us from receiving Him, for *He* is our Strength. This is why we must not let the devil deceive us. "Receive Communion often, *very often*," Thérèse writes. *This* is the "remedy" that brings healing![360]

In 1910, the diocesan process examining Thérèse's cause for canonization began. The vice postulator for Thérèse's cause, Msgr. de Teil, showed Pope St. Pius X this very letter of Thérèse to her cousin. De Teil noted that Thérèse's letter gave fitting support for Pius X's previous decree of 1905, *Sacra Tridentina*, encouraging frequent Communion. Her letter also provided marvelous support for the decree *Quam Singulari*, which the pope was about to publish. This decree permitted children at the age of reason, approximately seven years old, to receive Holy Communion and also encouraged children's *daily* reception of the Lord after their First Holy Communion. Pope St. Pius X received Thérèse's letter with great joy, noting that the cause for her canonization needed to be advanced quickly.[361] On June 10, 1914, two months before

---

[360] Ibid., pp. 568, 569.
[361] Ibid., p. 569.

his death, Pope St. Pius X gave approval for the beatification process for Thérèse to begin, and in 1915, the Apostolic Process was held. Pope St. Pius X's successor, Pope Pius XI, beatified Thérèse in 1923 and canonized her in 1925.

At the Apostolic Process, Sr. Marie of the Sacred Heart testified that being deprived of daily Communion was Thérèse's greatest trial during her years at Carmel. With so many others, Sr. Marie of the Sacred Heart was convinced that it was due to *Thérèse's* fervent intercession that Pope St. Pius X had granted to all the faithful, including young children, the privilege of receiving Holy Communion every day.[362]

We who today enjoy the magnificent blessing of being able to receive the Lord daily owe a great debt of gratitude to our beloved sister St. Thérèse. May her continued intercession gain for us ever-deepening love for the Lord, who offers us, every day of our lives, the precious gift of Himself.

St. John Vianney

In May 1925, when Pope Pius XI canonized Thérèse, he also canonized St. John-Marie Vianney, the curé, or parish priest, of the village of Ars, France. Like Thérèse, John Vianney was known for his profound love for the Lord in the Eucharist. He was a humble parish priest, not a writer, but his wonderful Eucharistic insights and counsels continue to touch the hearts of many people today.

St. John Vianney (1786–1859) was born in Dardilly, France, the fourth of six children. His family members were poor farmers, and John did not attend school but was taught at home. When he was seventeen, he realized that the Lord was calling him to

---

[362] Sr. Marie of the Sacred Heart, in *Witnesses of the Apostolic Canonization Process*, Witness Seven, 573.

be a priest. Without any formal education, however, he was not prepared for the academic rigors of seminary classes, which were all taught in Latin. He entered the seminary at Lyons and then was forced to leave. Enduring many struggles and trials during the following years, John received private tutoring as well as the heartfelt recommendation of a beloved priest and friend, and he finally was accepted for ordination in 1815.

For several years, John served as the assistant priest at a local parish. Then, in 1818, he was appointed to serve as the pastor in the small village of Ars, where very few seemed to be living their Catholic Faith. John labored, prayed, and sacrificed there, celebrating Mass daily and spending much energy preaching and teaching his people. His life was a simple one of poverty and caring for the poor, but the Holy Spirit also gave John an extraordinary gift of reading hearts. He often spent entire days in the confessional, with throngs of people coming to him, not only from Ars but also from distant cities. It was not unusual for people to wait long hours and even days for the opportunity to go to him for Confession.

John fostered among his people fervent devotion to our Blessed Mother and especially adoration of the Lord in the Blessed Sacrament as treasured means of growing close to the Lord. After forty years of ministering with complete selflessness to his parishioners and all those who came to him at Ars, John Vianney died on August 4, 1859. Pope Pius XI canonized him on May 31, 1925, and in 1929, he was named patron of parish priests. In 2010, Pope Benedict XVI named St. John Vianney the special patron of all priests.

The Wonders of the Mass

St. John Vianney was not a writer; his was the gift of speaking to the hearts of his people from his own heart, in a deeply practical and familiar way. His words bear the special anointing of the Holy

The Wonders of the Mass and the Eucharist

Spirit especially when he speaks to us about the Mass and the Blessed Sacrament. What a tremendous privilege is ours in being able to attend Mass, John assures us! Through the sacred ministry of His ordained bishops and priests, the mighty "wonders" that the Lord accomplished for us on Calvary He now makes present on the altars of our churches. And we are blessed beyond all imagining to be there![363] After Mass, if someone were to ask us where we have been, we can and should respond that we have been in *Heaven* and that we are bringing *Heaven* home with us![364]

Because the Mass is nothing less than the "work of God," St. John encourages us to come to church at least fifteen minutes before Mass begins. In this way, we will be able to prepare our minds and hearts to enter into the wonders in which we will be blessed to share. If we were told that a dead person we knew had just been raised to life, we would *run* to witness this glorious miracle! And yet, at the Consecration, through the ministry of the bishop or priest, a much more magnificent miracle than this takes place. If we truly understood that after the Consecration the Lord of Heaven and earth is present upon the altar, we would "die of love."[365]

St. John reminds us that we need faith to "see" the miracle of love that takes place at Mass. When the priest or bishop raises the sacred Host for our adoration after the Consecration, let us, like the blind man of Jericho, beg the Lord, "O Lord, make me *see!*" (see Luke 18:41). The Lord Jesus, whose arms are filled to overflowing with precious graces for us, will surely answer this prayer, which He Himself inspires within us.[366]

---

[363] St. John Baptist Mary Vianney, *The Eucharistic Meditations of the Curé d'Ars*, 19.1 (N.p.: Carmelite Publications, 1961), p. 23.

[364] Ibid., Meditation 18, Introduction, p. 22.

[365] St. John Vianney, *Catechetical Instructions*, chap. 10.

[366] Ibid., chap. 11.

When we receive the Lord in Holy Communion, He makes our hearts His throne. Such a tremendous honor requires that we show our respect and love for the Lord in our thoughts and our desires and in our outward demeanor and clothing.[367] John urges us to pray also that, when we return home after Mass, our thoughts, words, and actions will continue to glorify the Lord, who makes His Heaven in our souls as well as in our churches.[368]

The Great Privilege of Receiving Holy Communion

When St. John Vianney speaks of our receiving the Lord at Mass, he begins by reminding us first of how lavishly the Divine Persons of the Trinity have provided a glorious feast in nature to feed us and all creatures. What wonderful fruits and vegetables grow so plentifully throughout the world! But what about our spiritual soul? It, too, must have its food. And what is this food? Nothing less than God. "Ah! what a beautiful thought," John cries out! "The soul can feed on nothing but *God!*" Only God is enough for us; our soul "absolutely *requires*" God![369]

And how does the Father provide us with this food without which we cannot live? The Father has done for us what we could not have dared even to dream: He has given us His only Son's precious Body and Blood to be our soul's food, to *eat*. And to ensure that we would truly *hunger* for this food, the divine Persons of the Trinity have implanted in our very nature a vast and great desire that only the *infinite* God can satisfy. The *Eucharist* is what our souls crave. When we are in the presence of this beautiful Sacrament, let us not act like people dying of thirst on the banks of a river

---

[367] St. John Vianney, *Eucharistic Meditations*, 17.1; 17.2; pp. 21, 22.

[368] Ibid., 18.4; 19, introduction; p. 23.

[369] St. John Vianney, *Catechetical Instructions*, chap. 13.

overflowing with life-giving water! John urges us to stretch out our hands to receive the Lord Jesus in Holy Communion, to receive the One who alone satisfies our souls' thirst, the Lord who is our joy and our very *life*.[370]

"*Go to Communion*, my children; go to Jesus with love and confidence; go and *live* upon Him, in order to live for Him," St. John urges us. Let us never be so busy about many things that we have no time to spend with the Lord, who so tenderly invites us: "Come to me, all you that are weary and are carrying heavy burdens, and I will give you rest" (Matt. 11:28). How can we possibly resist this invitation filled with such infinite love and affection? Let us never think that, because we are unworthy, we dare not receive Him. Yes, we *are* unworthy; but we also are in *need*. If the Lord had considered only our unworthiness, John assures us, He would never have given us this precious Sacrament. If we refrain from receiving the Lord because we feel that we are unworthy, we are like people who are sick and who, precisely because they are sick, say they are not worthy to consult a doctor![371]

When we receive Holy Communion, John urges us to speak to the Lord as familiarly as did His disciples, who lived in His company. Let us tell the Lord Jesus of our love and ask Him, as our dearest Friend, for the blessings that we and our loved ones so desperately need. Rather than rushing out immediately after Mass, let us spend some time resting in the Lord's presence before we leave the church.[372]

With St. Thomas Aquinas, St. John Vianney reminds us of how infinitely *sweet* it is to be fed with God. How great is our

[370] Ibid., chap. 12.
[371] Ibid., chap. 13.
[372] St. John Vianney, *Eucharistic Meditations*, 18.2; 18.3; pp. 22, 23.

dignity that we are privileged to receive into our bodies the Body and Blood of the God of Heaven and earth! Everything in the Mass prepares us to receive the Lord in the Eucharist. And this is true of our entire lives as well. *Everything* in our lives should be preparing us to receive Jesus, who imparts to us His own sweetness and strength, His own peace and joy. Indeed, when we receive the Lord in Holy Communion, we truly are in "Heaven on earth."[373]

After Mass, if we are asked, "What are you carrying away to your home," John tells us to answer, "I am carrying away *Heaven!*" In a wonderfully sweet comment, John assures us that when we leave the Holy Banquet of the Mass, we should be even more ecstatic than the Magi would have been if they had been able to carry away with them the Baby Jesus—to keep! Receiving the Lord in Holy Communion fills our souls with such immense happiness and peace that, with St. John the beloved disciple, we cannot help crying out with gratitude and praise, "It is the Lord!" (John 21:7).[374] Yes, it *is* the Lord we are carrying away to our homes with us—and, through grace, to keep!

In another touching reflection, St. John Vianney describes how beautiful we will be in *Heaven* after we have feasted on earth on the precious Lamb of God as devoutly and as often as we could. John pictures how lovingly and sweetly our Blessed Mother and all the angels will rush to greet us as we enter Heaven! They will recognize in our souls the fragrance of their Lord, upon whom they, and we, have so often fed in the Eucharist, and they will see in us His own humility, charity, and peace. St. John Vianney also assures us that, after our resurrection at the end of time, the Lord's sacred Body and Blood will be especially radiant within us

---

[373] St. John Vianney, *Catechetical Instructions*, chap. 13.
[374] Ibid., chap. 12.

because of our having received the Lord so often. His precious Body will be shining in our bodies, and His precious Blood will be radiant in our blood.[375]

The Joy of Time with the Lord in the Blessed Sacrament

St. John Vianney asks us to recall how, throughout the ages, countless Christians have made pilgrimages to faraway cities in order to see the blessed places where the Lord suffered, died, and rose for us. Throngs of people have visited the Cenacle, where the Lord celebrated the Last Supper, and Calvary, where the Lord died for us. They have been moved to tears by being present at these blessed sites, in which their faith and love for the Lord have been deeply enkindled. And yet, St. John reminds us, we don't have to travel thousands of miles to be so profoundly moved by the Lord's love for us. We have *Him* in our churches, the *Lord Himself*, Body and Blood, Soul and Divinity! It is for this very reason that our churches are consecrated, because the Lord of Heaven and earth lives in them![376]

And what is the Lord of Heaven and earth doing in every tabernacle of the world, even as we neglect to visit Him, our dearest and most intimate Friend? He is loving us, pouring out His blessings upon us, inviting us to come to Him, to spend time with Him.[377] St. John Vianney calls to mind the homes of his time that had a cherished "store room" where the family's treasures were kept. The church is *our* home as Christians, and in our home is *our* sacred "store room" containing the most precious of all our treasures, the tabernacle in which the Lord Himself dwells.[378]

---

[375] Ibid., chap. 13.

[376] St. John Vianney, *Eucharistic Meditations*, 19.1; p. 23.

[377] Ibid., 20.1; p. 24.

[378] St. John Vianney, *Catechetical Instructions*, chap. 13.

St. John urges us in our every need to go to the Lord in
the Blessed Sacrament, for He is our most intimate and beloved
Friend and deepest comfort. When we are struggling with temptations, when we are discouraged and feeling hopeless and without
friends, when we are afraid and have nowhere to turn, let us go
to the Lord, who is our strength and joy. When we feel dry and
empty, let us go to Him, the overflowing font of every blessing.
And when we are weighed down with sin, feeling that there is no
hope for us, let us go to Him who is our pardon, our forgiveness,
and our peace.[379]

In the Blessed Sacrament, the Lord is physically present with
us, *always* loving us and interceding for us. Let us go to Him to
tell Him also of our gratitude and to intercede for our loved ones
and all those in need.[380] "How sweet and consoling" is this time
that we spend with the Lord, St. John Vianney cries out. In the
Lord's physical presence there is no boredom but only profound
peace that gives us a precious foretaste of Heaven here on earth.[381]

Yes, St. John assures us, the Lord in the Eucharist truly is
our "*Paradise*" on earth. He is joy in our sorrows, strength in our
weakness, comfort and peace in our trials, always ensuring that
everything in our lives turns out for our good (Rom. 8:28). How
blessed we are to be able to be *with* Him, *physically*, whenever we
want! When we are in the Lord's presence, we don't even need to
say much in order to pray. Let us simply rest in the Lord's heart
and enjoy just being close to Him. "That is the best prayer," St.
John assures us.[382]

---

[379] St. John Vianney, *Eucharistic Meditations*, 20.3; p. 25.
[380] Ibid., 20.4; p. 25.
[381] Ibid., 21.1; p. 26.
[382] Ibid., 21.2, 22; pp. 26, 27.

The Wonders of the Mass and the Eucharist

The Lord is always waiting for us in the Blessed Sacrament, waiting to console us, to forgive and heal us, to pour out His every blessing upon us. And how tremendously pleased He is when we *take time* to be with Him; how tenderly He smiles upon us! St. John Vianney assures us that the Lord loves us so dearly that it is as if He sees no one else in the universe but us! And if we could gaze upon the Lord as the angels do, we would fall so completely in love with Him that we would never want to leave Him. Just *being with* the Lord Jesus, being close to Him in the Blessed Sacrament, would be like Heaven itself. And it *is* Heaven, for we are in the presence of the *Lord*. How can we not cry out with Peter: "Lord, it is *good* for us to be here!" (Matt. 17:4).[383]

St. John Vianney tells the story of a man in his parish who always stopped to spend time with the Lord whenever he passed by a church. He would just go in to sit before the Lord in the Blessed Sacrament. When John asked him what he said to the Lord during his many visits, the man replied simply, "I say nothing. I look at Him, and He looks at me." "How beautiful, my children," St. John Vianney remarks.[384] Yes, how beautiful. As St. John Vianney assures us, we do not need many words to speak to the Lord in the Blessed Sacrament. Let us do as that dear man did who so touched the heart of St. John Vianney. With our hearts, let us simply look at the Lord with love and let Him look with infinite love at us.

[383] St. John Vianney, *Catechetical Instructions*, chap. 11.
[384] St. John Vianney, *Eucharistic Meditations*, 22; p. 27.

7

St. Alphonsus Liguori and St. John Paul II

Adoring the Lord in the Eucharist

In this final chapter, we meditate on the Eucharistic insights of St. Alphonsus Liguori and St. John Paul II. Blessed with tender hearts, both saints cherished a fervent love for Our Blessed Mother and longed to draw others close to the Lord in the Eucharist. With compassion deepened by suffering, both saints urge us to find in the Lord's Eucharistic presence the source of our joy and very life.

St. Alphonsus Mary Liguori

Born to a noble Italian family, Alphonsus Liguori (1696–1787) was known for his extraordinary intellectual gifts. The oldest of seven children of devout Catholic parents, he excelled in his studies as a youth and, at the age of sixteen, earned his doctorate in law from the University of Naples. By the age of twenty-one, Alphonsus had become the head of his own flourishing legal practice. He also was a gifted musician who loved playing the harpsichord and attending the opera. One day, however, he experienced a profound mystical grace in which he reevaluated his life and became attentive to the inspiration of the Holy Spirit calling him to consecrate his life to the Lord as a priest.

The Wonders of the Mass and the Eucharist

After his ordination in 1726 at the age of twenty-nine, Alphonsus spent six years preaching missions to the poorest and most neglected throughout the countryside of Naples. He was known and loved for his heartfelt preaching, compassion, and tenderness, especially with those who came to him burdened with sin and longing to be healed through the Sacrament of Confession.

In a special way, Alphonsus was drawn to the mystery of the redemption won for us by the sacred Passion and death of the Lord Jesus. The Holy Spirit filled Alphonsus with a longing to proclaim this saving mystery to all, especially to the poor and the most abandoned. Inspired by the Holy Spirit, and with the help of others close to him, in 1732 he founded the Congregation of the Most Holy Redeemer, the Redemptorists.

Despite suffering numerous trials, Alphonsus relied on the Holy Spirit's guidance and strength and continued to preach missions with compassion and love to poor people in the countryside. All the while, he dedicated much energy to writing spiritual and theological works to help and inspire others. A gifted artist and musician, Alphonsus also composed wonderful prayers and hymns that he would teach his people. His beloved Christmas carol "Tu Scendi Delle Stelle," composed in 1732, is sung throughout Italy today. The beautiful Stations of the Cross that he wrote in 1761 are still used in many Catholic churches during Lent. And countless Catholics pray Alphonsus's Act of Spiritual Communion when they are not able to be present at Mass.

In 1762, when he was sixty-six, Alphonsus was named bishop of Sant'Agata dei Goti. With all his strength, he devoted himself to instructing his people and to deepening their spiritual growth, even as he continued writing important spiritual, theological, and moral works. Within a short while after being named bishop, however, Alphonsus began to suffer from the debilitating arthritis that eventually would severely deform him. In 1775, after laboring as bishop for thirteen years, he begged to be relieved of his episcopal duties.

Alphonsus retired to the Redemptorist motherhouse at Pagani in Salerno. Struggling with the ravages of crippling arthritis, he also became increasingly deaf and blind, with his spine so curved that he could not stand. His entire body was so bent over to one side that it was impossible for him even to lift his head from his chest. As a result, a wound on his chest became infected, and the infection spread throughout his body. Because of his deformities, Alphonsus suffered constantly from sleepless nights, and, most painful of all, it became increasingly difficult and then impossible for him to celebrate Mass.

Confined to a wheelchair, Alphonsus eventually became completely dependent on the care of others. For years, he suffered excruciating physical, spiritual, and emotional trials, including struggles with scrupulosity and being mistreated and misunderstood by others. After enduring all these ordeals with resignation to the will of God, Alphonsus died peacefully in 1787 at the age of ninety-one. He was canonized in 1839, and his writings in spiritual and moral theology earned him the title of Doctor of the Church in 1871. Among the more than sixty works he wrote are his still well-loved *Visits to the Blessed Sacrament*, *The Glories of Mary*, and *The Practice of the Love of Jesus Christ*. St. Alphonsus, lover of the Lord in the Eucharist, is especially invoked as a patron of those suffering from debilitating diseases and emotional and mental trials.

The Lord's Closeness to Us in the Eucharist

Known for his gentleness and closeness to his people, Alphonsus was blessed with a brilliant mind, yet he also spoke and wrote in a simple, humble manner, desiring to help people in their everyday lives.[385] As he proclaimed the redeeming love of the Lord for us, Alphonsus was inseparably drawn also to His intimate closeness to us in the Blessed Sacrament. With deep warmth and affection, he preached and wrote about the Lord's unreserved giving of Himself to us in the Eucharist.

Alphonsus studied and loved the writings of the saints, whom he often quoted in his own writings on the Eucharist. In company with the saints before him, he was drawn especially to the mystery of the Last Supper. "What infinite tenderness!" St. Alphonsus exclaims. Longing to give Himself completely to us and in the most intimate way possible, the Lord "reduces himself to *food*" so that He can be not only with us but also *within* us, united to us even in His physicality.[386]

It is through the Eucharist, the great Sacrament of Love, that the Lord says to us, "You can never any more doubt that I love you, and love you to *excess*." When we receive the Lord, *everything* good comes to us together with Him. St. Alphonsus begs us not to let anything hold us back from receiving the precious Body and Blood of Jesus in the Eucharist. If we are in the state of serious sin, let us first seek out the healing grace of the Sacrament of Penance, but let us not refrain from receiving the Lord simply because we feel that we are unworthy. At every Mass, we pray, "Lord, I am *not* worthy that you should enter under my roof, but only say the word and my soul shall be healed" (cf. Luke 7:6-7). When we are cold, do we willingly keep ourselves away from the fire? When we feel

---

[385] St. John Paul II, *Spiritus Domini*, Apostolic Letter for the Bicentenary of the Death of St. Alphonsus De'Liguori, (August 1, 1987).

[386] St. Alphonsus Liguori, Meditation 5 for the Octave of Corpus Christi, in *The Holy Eucharist*, vol. 6 of *The Complete Ascetical Works of St. Alphonsus de Liguori*, ed. Eugene Grimm (New York: Benziger Brothers, 1887), p. 220.

unworthy, all the more should we receive this precious Sacrament with trust in the Lord's mercy, so that we may receive from the Lord the very fire of love that we lack.[387]

Alphonsus also begs us not to leave immediately after Mass but rather to spend some time with the Lord, who so longs to fill us with everything good. In a special way, let us cherish the gift of being held close to the Lord's heart after receiving Him. It is then that we can be most receptive to the wondrous "treasures of grace" that the Lord longs to pour out upon us.[388]

Prayer before the Blessed Sacrament

One of Alphonsus's most beautiful writings is his *Visits to the Blessed Sacrament*, written in 1745, when he was in his fifties. This was his very first book, and it was so compelling that forty editions of it were published even during his lifetime. This precious work, composed by Alphonsus and often drawn from writings of the saints, contains thirty-one days of meditations and prayers to the Lord in the Blessed Sacrament. In his introduction, Alphonsus writes that he hopes his readers will not "despise" his "little book," for he wrote it with the "utmost simplicity" in order to inspire devotion to the Eucharistic Lord in people of all walks of life.[389]

In *Visits to the Blessed Sacrament*, Alphonsus meditates on the tremendous comfort it gives us to spend time with the Lord in the Eucharist, speaking with Him "heart to heart." Jesus wants us to draw close to Him not only as our Lord and Savior but also as our

---

[387] St. Alphonsus Liguori, *The Practice of the Love of Jesus Christ*, introduction 2, in *The Holy Eucharist*, pp. 276, 282, 284.

[388] St. Alphonsus Liguori, Meditation 8 for the Octave of Corpus Christi, in *The Holy Eucharist*, p. 227.

[389] St. Alphonsus Liguori, *Visits to the Blessed Sacrament*, in *The Holy Eucharist*, p. 112.

most intimate *Friend*. We know how much it consoles us to take shelter in the warmth of our beloved friends. Infinitely more do we find comfort when we place our trust in the Lord and go to *Him* with all our troubles. Especially when we are in His Eucharistic presence, Jesus desires to bless us in the most tender ways, so that we may "taste and see" how good He is (Ps. 34:8).[390]

Alphonsus assures us that those who walked with the Lord, who ate with Him, who felt His healing touch and delighted in His tender gaze enjoyed no advantage over us today. The Lord Himself has promised us, "I am with you *always*" (Matt. 28:20). Do we really believe this—that the Lord who walked this earth, who suffered and died and rose for us, is the very same Lord who dwells *physically* with us in the Blessed Sacrament? Because we have His intimate, physical presence with and within us, comforting, helping, and loving us, we can enjoy the consolation of His presence as surely as His disciples did when they wanted just to be close to Him.[391]

No other treasure on earth is more worthy of our love than Jesus in the Eucharist. This is why Alphonsus urges us to spend time with the Lord in the Blessed Sacrament whenever we can: before and after Mass, during visits to the church, or during Eucharistic adoration. In this great Sacrament of Love, the Lord Himself is *physically* present with us and longs to pour out upon us His most intimate blessings. It is also while we are adoring the Lord in the Eucharist that the Holy Spirit makes us especially docile to His inspirations. St. Alphonsus tells us that it was while he was praying before the Blessed Sacrament that he received the grace to respond wholeheartedly to the Lord's call to him to be a priest.[392]

---

[390] Ibid., introduction, 1, p. 118.
[391] Ibid., Nineteenth Visit to the Blessed Sacrament, p. 171.
[392] Ibid., introduction, 1, pp. 116, 117.

Jesus *delights* to be intimately, physically with us; may we find *our* delight in being with *Him*! In all our problems and trials, Alphonsus urges us to go to the Lord in the Eucharist. When we are suffering, when we feel miserable, let us go to Jesus, who is our healing, our comfort, and our strength. Let us not waste time being disheartened and discouraged. Instead, Alphonsus urges us, let us run straight to the Lord, our beloved Friend, who wants to and *can* make well all that is not well within us. To every one of us He says these precious words: "Come to *me* ... and I will give you rest" (Matt. 11:28). The Lord Himself is inviting us, "Bring your every need to *me*. Place all your trust in me, and let me hold you close to my heart." Alphonsus encourages us to respond to Jesus from our hearts, just as Mary and Martha, the sisters of Lazarus, did: "Lord, the one You love is sick" (see John 11:3). "Yes, Lord," let us say to Him. "*I* am the whom you love, and *I* am the one who is sick. I come to You to rest on Your heart and to be healed."[393]

Alphonsus reminds us of how sweet it is to be physically close to those we love. Often, we don't even need to say anything; it makes us happy just to be with them. How much sweeter it is to be with Jesus, who loves us more tenderly than we can imagine. What comfort and grace would fill us if, whenever we can, we would spend even a few moments in the Lord's presence, simply letting Him *love us*. Jesus, our Lord and God, longs to fill us with everything good, but no words can express how sweet it is just to be *with* Him, to be *close* to Him. We can go to Him at any time and tell Him about all our needs. We can be completely ourselves, hiding nothing, holding nothing back, opening our hearts to Him who is so intimately present with us in the Blessed Sacrament. What

---

[393] Ibid., Third, Eighth, and Sixteenth Visits, pp. 133, 144, 163–164.

a comfort it is simply to rest on His heart, as the beloved disciple did at the Last Supper (see John 13:23).[394]

There was a Carmelite brother, Alphonsus tells us, who would go in and spend time with the Lord in the Blessed Sacrament every time he passed a church. The brother would say that it was "not becoming" for a friend to pass by the door of a friend without stopping to see him for even a few moments. Let us, then, go to the Lord in the Blessed Sacrament as to our beloved and dearest friend. If we would spend even a little time with the Eucharistic Lord whenever we can, we would find the remedy for every one of our troubles. Again, Alphonsus reminds us that Jesus longs for us to be with Him: "Come to me, all you who are weary … and I will give you rest" (Matt. 11:28). Instead of becoming bitter and discouraged by our trials, let us go to the arms of Jesus, who has the power to make well all that is disturbing our peace of soul.[395]

Throughout the entire world, the Lord remains on our altars night and day so that we may easily find Him. Alphonsus encourages us to go to Him to be consoled, to be filled with His peace and strength, and to receive into our inmost being the tremendous blessings He longs to bestow on us.[396]

Alphonsus also reminds us that the Lord has no need of us; He is infinitely happy without our love. And yet He loves us so passionately that He wants to be with us, physically, not only as He was during the years when He walked this earth, but always. We could ask what more He could possibly do for us after the astounding wonders of His life, Passion, death, Resurrection, Ascension,

---

[394] Ibid., Seventeenth and Nineteenth Visits, pp. 165, 170.
[395] Ibid., Twentieth, Thirty-First, and Sixteenth Visits, pp. 174, 205, 163.
[396] St. Alphonsus Liguori, Meditation 2 for the Octave of Corpus Christi, in *The Holy Eucharist*, p. 215.

and pouring out the Holy Spirit at Pentecost, all for our sake. But the Lord *did* want to do even more for us: He wanted never to deprive us of His *physical* closeness. And so, in the precious sacrament of the Eucharist, He has given us *Himself*. Why? Because, Alphonsus assures us, He "cannot bear to separate himself from us." "Those who eat my flesh and drink my blood, *abide* in me and I in them" (John 6:56). Unworthy though we are, we are still the Lord's *delight*, and He longs to be completely united to us, to make His heart and ours as *one*.[397]

Spending Time with Jesus after Holy Communion

At no time are we closer to Jesus than after Holy Communion, and no prayer is dearer to Him than our prayer to Him after we receive Him in the Eucharist. Alphonsus recalls a beautiful insight of St. Teresa of Ávila: coming to us in Holy Communion, Jesus makes our souls His "throne of grace" and tenderly invites us to confide to Him our every need and longing. The Lord *wants* us to ask Him for anything we need, and He *loves* to grant our prayers, especially at this most intimate of times, as we rest on His heart after Holy Communion. In ways infinitely better than we could imagine, Jesus *will* grant the deepest desires of our hearts, if not always in the way we want, always in the way we most deeply need. Alphonsus again urges us not to waste the precious time after Holy Communion by leaving Mass immediately. Let us spend time resting on the Lord's heart, letting Him love us and confiding to Him all our needs and deepest longings.[398]

---

[397] St. Alphonsus Liguori, Novena to the Sacred Heart, Meditations 3 and 2, in *The Holy Eucharist*, pp. 240, 238.

[398] St. Alphonsus Liguori, Meditation 8 for the Octave of Corpus Christi, in *The Holy Eucharist*, p. 227.

The Wonders of the Mass and the Eucharist

Throughout the years, St. Alphonsus himself surely learned to do this more and more deeply, entrusting to the Lord in the Eucharist all his trials and problems. It was while he was still ministering as bishop, and after he began to suffer more intensely from arthritic disease, that, in 1768, he wrote *The Practice of the Love of Jesus Christ*. His insights on the Eucharist in this beautiful work reflect the understanding and gratitude that suffering had served to deepen in him.

Alphonsus asks us to contemplate all the beautiful realities we experience in our created world: the wonders of nature, the treasure of loved ones, the gifts of mind and heart and soul with which we are blessed. All these created gifts inspire our love and gratitude. Most of all, however, the Lord's excruciating death for us on the Cross should draw forth from us our undying gratitude. And yet, even dying for us was not enough for Him. Jesus wanted to show His infinite love for us in a way that we would never forget, in a way that would make it impossible for us to consider His sufferings for us as past and done with. The Lord's undying love impelled Him not only to die for us but also, and even more, to give us His precious Body, tortured for us, and His precious Blood, poured out for us, as our food and drink.[399]

St. Thomas Aquinas's tender name for the Eucharist, "the Sacrament of love," was especially dear to Alphonsus.[400] Infinite love alone impelled Jesus to give us *Himself*, Body and Blood, Soul and Divinity, in this way, saying to us: "*Now* you can never doubt that I love you to *excess*." Yes, to excess! We could never imagine that the God of Heaven and earth would become flesh of our

---

[399] St. Alphonsus Liguori, *The Practice of the Love of Jesus Christ*, introduction, 1 and 4, in *The Holy Eucharist*, pp. 265, 296.

[400] St. Thomas Aquinas, *Summa Theologiae*, III.73.3, ad 3.

flesh in the mystery of His Incarnation or that the Lord of Lords would undergo an excruciating death by crucifixion for love of us. Even more, we could never dream of the wondrous mystery of the Lord's giving us His most precious Body and Blood to *eat* in the Eucharist. Many of His disciples refused to believe the Lord when He spoke of this miracle of His love: "How can this man give us his flesh to eat.... This saying is difficult; who can accept it?" (John 6:52, 60). And yet what we could never conceive, or even dare to dream, Jesus Himself does for us: "Take, *eat*, this *is* my body" (Matt. 26:26).[401]

To keep our minds and hearts centered on the Lord after we have received Him, St. Alphonsus tells us that the Holy Spirit may inspire us simply to repeat phrases from hymns and prayers that are dear to our hearts, such as the beautiful Anima Christi: "Soul of Christ, sanctify me; Body of Christ, protect me; Blood of Christ, inebriate me." In this prayer, we also beg the Lord, "O good Jesus,... within Your wounds, hide me.... In my last hour call me and bid me come to You."[402] Here we are reminded of St. Bernard of Clairvaux's exquisite expression of love for the Lord: "Jesus to me is honey in the mouth, music in the ear, a song in the heart!" If His precious *name* is the healing medicine for our every trial, and has the power to lift us even from the depths of despair,[403] how much more so is this true of the Lord *Himself* present in the Eucharist!

When we are not able to receive the Lord in Holy Communion, Alphonsus encourages us to make acts of *spiritual* Communion by

---

[401] St. Alphonsus Liguori, *The Practice of the Love of Jesus Christ*, introduction, 2, in *The Holy Eucharist*, pp. 276, 277.

[402] St. Alphonsus Liguori, Acts after Holy Communion, in *The Holy Eucharist*, p. 82.

[403] St. Bernard of Clairvaux, *On the Song of Songs*, Sermon 15.6.

telling Jesus that we *desire* to receive Him. In this way, throughout the day, we can be close to the Lord in the Eucharist and deepen our love for Him.[404] Both when we receive the Lord in Holy Communion and when we make acts of spiritual Communion throughout the day, let us give ourselves completely to Him who gives Himself so unreservedly to us. And, as the Lord holds us always close to His heart, let us, too, hold Him always close to our hearts, asking Him to make our souls more and more His sweet Heaven and home (John 14:23).[405]

In his introduction to *Visits to the Blessed Sacrament*, Alphonsus asked his readers to pray to the Lord in the Blessed Sacrament for him. In return, he promised to pray for his readers every time he offered the Holy Sacrifice of the Mass.[406] Now that he is honored by the entire Church as a saint in Heaven, surely Alphonsus prays even more powerfully for us as we beg his intercession and ponder his insights on how beautiful it is to draw close to the Lord in the Eucharist.

Pope St. John Paul II

St. Alphonsus was blessed with a loving heart and a burning desire to inflame others with love for the Lord in the Eucharist. These same wonderful characteristics shone in St. John Paul II. The pope himself admired St. Alphonsus's affectionate love, which enabled him to become a dear and "close friend" to his people.[407]

---

[404] St. Alphonsus Liguori, *The Practice of the Love of Jesus Christ*, 4.4, in *The Holy Eucharist*, pp. 349, 351.

[405] St. Alphonsus Liguori, *Loving Aspirations to Jesus in the Blessed Sacrament*, 6, 8, in *The Holy Eucharist*, pp. 87, 89.

[406] St. Alphonsus Liguori, *Visits to the Blessed Sacrament*, in *The Holy Eucharist*, p. 112.

[407] St. John Paul II, *Spiritus Domini*.

In addition, the compassion of both saints was refined in the crucible of physical, mental, and emotional suffering. While St. Alphonsus is an advocate for those afflicted with arthritic disease and emotional trials, St. John Paul II is an intercessor for those who suffer from familial losses and neurological disorders such as Parkinson's disease.

The future Pope John Paul II, Karol Józef Wojtyła, was born in the Polish town of Wadowice, near Kraków, on May 18, 1920. His older sister died before he was born. Karol also suffered the death of his mother when he was only nine and the death of his older brother, a doctor, when he was twelve. It was his beloved father who raised him and fostered in him a deeply spiritual life.

After graduating from high school, Karol enrolled in Kraków's Jagiellonian University in 1938. The university, however, closed the next year because of the Nazi occupation, and Karol obtained work in a quarry and then in a chemical factory. After his father's death in 1941, he became convinced that he was called to be a priest. In 1942, under the auspices of the archbishop of Kraków, he began to study secretly for the priesthood in the underground seminary at Kraków. When World War II ended, Karol openly resumed his seminary education and studied theology at Jagiellonian University.

In 1946, Karol was ordained a priest in Kraków and soon afterward was sent to Rome to study with the French Dominican Réginald Garrigou-Lagrange. After completing his doctorate in theology in 1948, Karol returned to Kraków to minister to university students and to serve as pastor in parish churches. In 1949, Fr. Karol began to teach ethics at Jagiellonian University and then at the Catholic University of Lublin. As a wonderful extension of his teaching ministry, he gathered a group of young people who called themselves *Rodzinka*, the "little family." They met for prayer, philosophical and theological discussions, and service to help those in need. Eventually, their time together included recreational activities such as annual skiing and kayaking trips.

Devoted groups of students began to meet with Fr. Karol regularly for weekends of retreat, prayer, discussion, and recreation together. He would celebrate outdoor Masses for his "little family," hold spiritual and theological discussions with them, and engage in outdoor sports such as hiking, skiing, bicycling, camping, and kayaking. In Russian-controlled Poland, priests were forbidden to travel with students. Fr. Karol asked his student companions and friends to call him *Wujek* (Uncle), a cherished nickname that began to be used also by others who knew and loved Fr. Karol.

In 1958, Pope Pius XII chose Fr. Karol to serve as auxiliary bishop of Kraków. Some friends were concerned that his responsibilities would cause him to become less familiar and more formal toward them. Fr. Karol assured them, "Wujek will *remain* Wujek." Even after his ordination as bishop in Wawel Cathedral, Kraków, Bishop Karol continued to live a very simple, familial life, and his friends and companions continued to call him, affectionately, Wujek. Pope St. Paul VI was among those who recognized Bishop Karol's profound spiritual, theological, and personal gifts, and, in 1964, he appointed him archbishop of Kraków. After Bishop Karol played a significant role at Vatican Council II (1962–1965), Pope Paul VI honored him again, naming him a cardinal in 1967.

Even with his pressing responsibilities, Karol continued to nurture affectionate friendships with those to whom the Lord drew him close. He was especially close in mind and heart with Mother Teresa of Calcutta, whose spiritual presence and intercessory prayer he keenly felt. Another dear friend was the Polish-born philosopher Anna-Teresa Tymieniecka, wife of Harvard University professor Hendrik Houthakker. In the summer of 1976, when Cardinal Karol traveled with a delegation of Polish bishops for a conference in the United States, Anna-Teresa invited him to stay with her family in Vermont. Karol greatly enjoyed the opportunity to spend time with his dear friend, taking pleasure in heartfelt discussions and outdoor activities such as hiking and kayaking.[408] Surely, blessed friendships such as these, which refreshed and uplifted John Paul II and other saints as well, encourage us to take time to enjoy the Lord's gift of our families and friends and to savor in a special way spending time with the Lord in the Eucharist.

Two years after his visit to Vermont, Cardinal Karol traveled to Rome to vote in the papal conclave after the death of Pope Paul VI. Pope John Paul I was elected, but he died after only thirty-three days as pope. Another papal conclave was held, and, in October 1978, Karol himself was elected pope. He took the name John Paul II to honor both his immediate predecessor and Pope Paul VI. In contrast to the exceedingly brief reign of Pope John Paul I, John Paul II's ministry as pope was one of the longest in the history of the Church, lasting nearly twenty-seven years.

The enormous accomplishments of this deeply loved pope cannot be summarized in a brief space. Throughout the years, love impelled him to greet and address more than seventeen million pilgrims in the General Audiences he held every Wednesday. His dedication to young people inspired him to establish the famed World Youth Days. The pope's missionary zeal resulted in his becoming a revered spiritual leader who traveled to numerous countries, meeting heads of nations and leaders of world religions.

---

[408] Joaquina Pires-O'Brien, "Anna-Teresa Tymieniecka and Her Friendship with Pope John Paul II," *PortVitoria* 21 (July–December 2020), https://portvitoria.com/anna-teresa-tymieniecka-and-her-friendship-with-pope-john-paul-ii/.

The Wonders of the Mass and the Eucharist

Mikhail Gorbachev acknowledged the pope's instrumental role in the fall of Communism in Central and Eastern Europe in 1989.

In countless ways, Pope John Paul II fostered the spiritual growth of the Church. His many writings include profoundly theological and spiritual letters and exhortations, apostolic constitutions, fourteen encyclicals, and several books. In weekly audiences from 1979 to 1984, he gave enormously influential instructions on his "Theology of the Body," and in 1992, he promulgated the *Catechism of the Catholic Church*. Proclaiming three Trinitarian years of preparation, the pope inspired the entire Church to celebrate with joy the Great Jubilee of the year 2000.

When he had begun to serve as pope in 1978, John Paul II was fifty-eight years old and in his prime. An avid sportsman from his youth, he remained extremely active—jogging, swimming, hiking, playing football, and kayaking. Over the years, however, and especially after being severely injured in an assassination attempt in 1981, the pope began to suffer from serious health issues. In the 1990s, his decline was noticeable, and in 2001, the pope was diagnosed with Parkinson's disease. In the following years, his ability to walk and to speak became more and more impaired. The pope suffered intensely, especially from the limitations affecting his movement and speech, and it became increasingly difficult for him to breathe.

In February 2005, the pope was rushed to the hospital to undergo a tracheotomy, and on March 31, 2005, Vatican officials confirmed that he was nearing death. Because of the pope's desire not to go back to the hospital, medical equipment was brought to his Vatican residence, where he was cared for by skilled physicians. Tens of thousands of people held vigil in St. Peter's Square and throughout Rome for two days. In the evening of April 2, 2005, the vigil of the feast of Divine Mercy, Pope John Paul II died, having begged those who kept watch with him to let him go home to his Father. His funeral was held on April 8, 2005, with countless people gathered and millions more watching the broadcast throughout the world. Almost immediately, people began to acclaim him a saint, calling him "John Paul the Great." Pope John Paul II was beatified in May 2011 by Pope Benedict XVI and was canonized by Pope Francis in 2014.

Pope John Paul II and the Corpus Christi Processions

The pope's tender love for the Lord in the Blessed Sacrament was nurtured in his childhood in Poland, especially as he learned to treasure the wonderful Corpus Christi processions in his homeland. In a cherished tradition that continues today, immense crowds of devout men, women, and children, dressed in colorful folk costumes, pay honor to the Blessed Sacrament, solemnly carried through the streets of Polish cities such as Wadowice, Łowicz, Kraków, and Łódź. In Rome, the pope did not lose his love for these processions. Encouraging as many people as possible to join in the Eucharistic processions in Rome on the feast of Corpus Christi, the pope made it a practice to give special homilies each year on this beautiful feast.

In his Corpus Christi homilies, the pope expresses his joy in this tremendous feast and urges us to participate in the beautiful "public devotions" honoring the Lord on this day. The pope had a special love for the Eucharistic poetry of St. Thomas Aquinas and often quoted him in his Corpus Christi homilies. Thomas's Eucharistic hymns express with "inspired transport" the most wonderful sentiments of adoration and love for the Lord's precious Body and Blood. As we have seen, these hymns are still cherished and used by the entire Church at Benediction and on the glorious feasts of Holy Thursday and Corpus Christi. The pope encourages us to nurture Thomas's sentiments of love and adoration before the Eucharistic Lord, crying out to Him in the words of Thomas's beautiful prayer "Adoro Te Devote:" "To You, O Lord, my whole heart is surrendered." The pope also inspires us to join our own gratitude and praise to Thomas's prayers and hymns, which the Church uses to celebrate the Eucharistic Lord throughout the world.[409]

With profound adoration, the pope notes, Thomas Aquinas lauds the Lord's infinite love at His Last Supper, giving us the sacred gift of His own sacred Body and Blood. How can this precious mystery not evoke from us the most profound adoration? Even the Church's most beautiful Eucharistic hymns and devotions cannot adequately express the glorious wonder of the Lord's presence in the Blessed Sacrament.[410]

John Paul II shares with us the joy of his own heart in the public nature of the honor paid to the Lord through Eucharistic processions. As they accompany the Eucharist, the faithful who participate in Corpus Christi processions join in spirit with countless people throughout the entire world. With praise and worship, they accompany the Blessed Sacrament carried in honor through the city streets, "close by the buildings where people live, rejoice and suffer." In this way, the Eucharistic Lord is *publicly* brought near to His people, to their lives and problems, their concerns and troubles, their worries and joys. On the feast of Corpus Christ, the entire Church celebrates and bears the Eucharist on the streets of cities and towns in every part of the world. The Church does this as a way to proclaim publicly that the Eucharist is the very source of her life and of the whole world's salvation. In Eucharistic

---

[409] St. John Paul II, Corpus Christi Homily, May 29, 1997, nos. 3, 4.
[410] St. John Paul II, Corpus Christi Homily, June 11, 1998, no. 3.

processions, the Lord especially pours out His mercy on those who accompany Him and also on the people whose homes and workplaces are blessed by His presence.[411]

"Tantum ergo Sacramentum veneremur cernui:" "Let us *fall down in adoration* before so great a sacrament," St. Thomas Aquinas had sung. In the Eucharist, the pope explains, the Lord Himself is *with* us, the very same Lord Jesus who walked this earth with His disciples, who was crucified and rose from the dead, the same risen Jesus before whom the apostle Thomas bowed in adoration and cried out, "My Lord and my God!" (John 20:28).[412] And because the Eucharist contains the "entire mystery" of the Lord's love, this wondrous sacrament is also inseparable from the Communion of Saints. As St. John Paul II assures us, when we receive the Lord in the Eucharist, we are united intimately to Him and, therefore, in a profound way, also united to one another on earth and to all those in Heaven, especially our loved ones.[413]

What is wonderful about the feast of Corpus Christi is that we are able to celebrate, together and without restraint, the profound mystery of Holy Thursday. As the prelude to the Lord's Passion, Holy Thursday itself evokes from us a solemn celebration. In contrast, Pope John Paul II notes, on the feast of Corpus Christi, we are able to celebrate the mystery of the Eucharist with unrestrained joy. The beautiful feast of Corpus Christi gives us the blessed opportunity to praise and celebrate and carry publicly through our streets the Church's "most precious treasure," the Lord *Himself*. This is the gift "surpassing all praise," whose mystery is so

---

[411] St. John Paul II, Corpus Christi Homily, June 22, 2000, no. 4; Corpus Christi Homily, June 10, 2004, no. 2.

[412] St. John Paul II, Corpus Christi Homily, June 14, 2001, no. 3.

[413] St. John Paul II, Corpus Christi Homily, June 19, 2003, nos. 2, 4.

"sublime," so "ineffable," that it evokes from us not only profound adoration but also ecstatic jubilation.[414]

Eucharistic Encyclical Ecclesia de Eucharistia:
We Draw Our Life from the Eucharist

Pope John Paul II sought to draw the Church to a deeper love for the Eucharist, not only through His Corpus Christi homilies but also through a beautiful document that was his very last encyclical: *Ecclesia de Eucharistia*. The title of this encyclical, taken from the opening sentence of its Latin text, expresses its profound theme: "The Church draws her life from the Eucharist." The Lord's precious Body and Blood is the Church's sacred food, without which she cannot live. The pope opens his heart to us, telling us that in this encyclical he wants to express publicly his own gratitude and profound "amazement" before the Sacrament of the Eucharist. His great desire is to enkindle in the entire Church a deeper worship and amazement before the Eucharist, which he again calls the Church's "most precious Treasure."[415]

The pope tells us that he felt compelled to unite with the whole Church in adoration before this great "mystery of mercy," for the Eucharist is the most wonderful gift the Lord could possibly give us, *Himself*. "What more could Jesus have done for us?" In giving us His own Body to eat and His own Blood to drink, He goes to the very "end" to which love can go (John 13:1), a love that is not satisfied even by His suffering an excruciating death on the Cross for us but only by His giving Himself *completely to us*.[416]

---

[414] St. John Paul II, Corpus Christi Homily, June 14, 2001, nos.1, 2.
[415] St. John Paul II, encyclical letter *Ecclesia de Eucharistia* (April 17, 2003), nos. 3, 6, 9.
[416] Ibid., 1.11.

And this He did at the Last Supper, which was both a *meal* of love and also the Lord's *sacrifice* of love. For Jesus did not simply *say* over the bread and wine these sacred words: "This is my Body"; "this is my Blood." Inseparably, He added, "which is *given* for you"; "which is *poured out* for you" (Luke 22:19–20). By adding these latter words, the Lord made clear the *sacrificial* nature of this sacred meal. At the Last Supper, the pope explains, the Lord "made sacramentally present" His sacrifice of love, which He would offer on the Cross the next day. Now, at Mass, through the ministry of His ordained bishops and priests, the Lord makes present to us His past Last Supper and, inseparably, His saving death and Resurrection.[417]

As the saints have stressed, without the Lord's death and Resurrection, there would be no Mass, and without the Mass, there would be no Eucharist. In a Communion Service, we receive the Eucharist as the sacred fruit of an already celebrated Mass. Although a Communion service is a beautiful liturgical service, it can never take the place of the Mass, for only in the Mass does the Lord make present to us His Last Supper, death, and Resurrection. St. John Chrysostom assures us that the Lord's sacrifice on the Cross and the Mass today are the *one same* sacrifice. The pope stresses that it is from this "redeeming sacrifice" of the Lord on the Cross that the entire Church draws its very life.[418] The deepest purpose of the Mass, however, is that we may receive the Lord's life *within* us, that we may *eat* His precious Body and *drink* His sacred Blood which He sacrificed for us on the Cross: "Unless you *eat* the flesh of the Son of Man and *drink* his blood, you have

---

[417] Ibid., 1.12; 1.14.
[418] Ibid., 1.12; St. John Chrysostom, Homily 17 on the Epistle to the Hebrews, 3.

no life within you" (John 6:53). Ah, John Paul II cries out, before such an infinite "mystery of love," how can we not bend low in adoration![419]

The pope also was struck by the Eucharistic *epiclesis*, in which the bishop or priest invokes the Holy Spirit upon the gifts of bread and wine. He was especially touched by the beautiful epiclesis in the Divine Liturgy of St. John Chrysostom. The Holy Spirit is invoked upon the bread and wine and *also* upon all the people present, so that "those who partake" of the divine Mysteries may be purified, their sins may be forgiven, and they may "share in the Holy Spirit." Our receiving the Lord's precious Body and Blood thus also deepens our union with the Holy Spirit and with the Father, to whom the Sacrifice of the Mass is offered.[420]

Amazing mystery of love! Our devoutly receiving the Lord in the Eucharist increases our intimacy through grace with the entire Trinity, in this way fulfilling a profound longing within us. The pope stresses the beautiful truth that we have been created by the Divine Persons of the Trinity, who are the infinite Family of Love. For this very reason, there is a longing deep within us truly to *belong* to our very own family, who cherish us and enfold us in their love. Surely, the pope himself, who had suffered the deaths of almost all of his immediate family when he was young, experienced this longing deep in his soul. John Paul II assures us that this desire within us for close, loving family life is fulfilled in the most intimate way possible by our union with our truest Family of Love, the Blessed Trinity, from whom all devoted family life draws its origin, purpose, and fulfillment. And this is what happens when we lovingly receive the Lord in the Eucharist: our

---

[419] St. John Paul II, *Ecclesia de Eucharistia*, 1.15; 1.16.
[420] Ibid., 1.17.

longing also for intimate family life is satisfied in the most profound way possible.[421]

Inseparably, our receiving the Lord in the Eucharist intimately unites us to those present with us at Mass, especially those dear to us. With our loved ones beside us, we receive Jesus, the Lord of love, who unites us to one another in a way infinitely deeper than anything our own efforts could accomplish. We are truly one in the *Lord*. Partaking together of the "one Bread" of the Eucharist, we become "one body" in Him (1 Cor. 10:17).[422] How profoundly this mystery is experienced, for example, not only by spouses and families but also by couples who receive the Sacrament of Marriage within the celebration of the Mass. Before they become "one body" in the sealing of their sacrament, they receive together the one Body of the Lord Jesus in the Eucharist, who makes them one in *His* own self-giving love.

Another truth that touched the pope's heart is that, because of the Lord in the Eucharist, we do not have to wait until the moment of death to possess eternal life. "Those who eat my flesh and drink my blood *have* eternal life" (John 6:54). Church Fathers such as St. Ignatius of Antioch tell us that the Eucharist is the powerful "antidote" for our death, the wonderful "Medicine of Immortality." Because the Eucharist *is* the risen Lord, the pope assures us, "with the Eucharist we 'digest,' as it were, the 'secret' of the resurrection." The Eucharist is the "anticipation of heaven," the "pledge of future glory" giving us in a profound way eternal life even here on earth.[423]

Raised by his devout and loving father, the pope surely longed to know again the joys of a full and complete family life, as he

[421] Ibid., 2.24.
[422] Ibid.
[423] Ibid., 1.18; St. Ignatius of Antioch, *Epistle to the Ephesians*, 20.

looked forward to when he would be united with all of his dear family in Heaven. We can understand the profound consolation John Paul II felt as he assures us that the Lord in the Eucharist intimately unites us to our loved ones on earth and *also* to those in Heaven, including those dear to us.[424] The pope recalls how, in the Eucharistic Prayers of both East and West, honor is given to Our Blessed Mother, the angels, the apostles, the martyrs, and all the saints. The Mass and the Eucharist unite us to the great Communion of Saints in Heaven, as we are joined intimately to the saints and angels who ceaselessly praise the crucified and risen Lord (Rev. 7:10).[425]

Devoutly participating in Mass and receiving the Lord in the Eucharist not only deepen our longing for Heaven but also inspire us to serve one another and, in our own ways, to work for deeper justice and peace in the world. Pope John Paul II assures us that it is not by accident that John's Gospel has no account of the Lord's institution of the Eucharist at the Last Supper. Instead, the Evangelist recounts the Lord's washing of His apostles' feet, in this way showing us the profound *meaning* of the Eucharist. We receive the Lord Jesus, who humbled Himself, who *sacrificed* and *gave* Himself for us. The Eucharistic Lord *wants* us to work for the good of one another, to labor, in whatever ways we can, to build a better world. "I wish to reaffirm this forcefully," the pope stresses. In the Eucharist, we receive the Lord, who fills us with His own love so that we may become instruments of His love and peace in our world. It is in this way that our lives become completely "Eucharistic."[426]

[424] St. John Paul II, *Ecclesia de Eucharistia*, 1.19.
[425] Ibid.
[426] Ibid., 1.19; 1:20.

We must never forget, however, that the Lord in the Eucharist is not a means to an end. The Lord *Himself* is worthy of all our love and adoration. This is why our participating in Mass, receiving the Lord in the Eucharist, and praying before the Blessed Sacrament are of "inestimable value for the life of the Church." Eucharistic adoration is an especially wonderful fruit of the Mass, ceaselessly drawing us back to the Mass and to our receiving the Lord sacramentally in the Eucharist.[427]

Pope John Paul II confides to us that he knows by experience how "pleasant" it is to "spend time" with the Eucharistic Lord, "to lie close to his breast like the beloved disciple (John 13:23) and to feel the infinite love present in his heart." It is a precious and intimate grace simply to be in the presence of the Lord of Heaven and earth, adoring and loving Him in the Blessed Sacrament. "How often, dear brothers and sisters, have I experienced this, and drawn from it strength, consolation and support!" The pope tells us that among the saints who inspire us by their love for the Lord in the Eucharist, he was especially touched by St. Alphonsus Liguori. He recalls the saint's beautiful comment that, after receiving the sacraments, particularly the Eucharist, Eucharistic adoration is the devotion "most pleasing to God and the one most useful to us."[428]

Apostolic Letter Mane Nobiscum Domine: *Stay with Us, Lord*

On October 7, 2004, Pope John Paul II published his last Eucharistic writing, *Mane Nobiscum Domine*, proclaiming the Year of the Eucharist. It was during this year, on April 2, 2005, that the pope, who so deeply loved the Eucharistic Lord, was called

---

[427] Ibid., 2:25.
[428] Ibid.; St. Alphonsus Liguori, *Visits to the Blessed Sacrament*, introduction, in *The Holy Eucharist*, p. 116.

home to Heaven. In his beautiful apostolic letter, the pope tells us what a profound grace it was for him to invite the entire Church to celebrate with him the wonders of the Eucharist. With all his soul, he longed to inspire in every one of us a deeper appreciation and love for the "incomparable treasure" the Lord has given us in the Eucharist.[429]

How prophetic and touching are the title and theme that the pope chose for his apostolic letter: *Mane Nobiscum Domine*, "Remain with Us, Lord." As two beloved disciples traveled to Emmaus, the Risen Lord appeared and walked along with them. Overcome by the tender power of His presence, but not yet recognizing Him, they could not endure being parted from him: "*Stay with us*, because it is almost evening" (Luke 24:29). The Lord did stay with them, and they recognized Him "in the breaking of the bread" (Luke 24:35).[430]

For Pope John Paul II, this passage confirms how the Eucharist has "*always* been at the center of the Church's life." Luke tells us that the early Church "devoted" itself "to the apostles' teaching and fellowship, to *the breaking of bread* and the prayers" (Acts 2:42). The "Breaking of the Bread": this is the name that the early Church gave to the Eucharistic celebration. It is precisely through the celebration of the Eucharist, the Mass, that the Lord has continued throughout the ages to make "present within time the mystery of his death and resurrection." And in the most precious fruit of the Mass, the Eucharist, the Lord gives Himself completely to us as the "living bread come down from heaven" (see John 6:51). These truths make us realize that, when we receive the Lord in

---

[429] St. John Paul II, apostolic letter *Mane Nobiscum Domine* for the Year of the Eucharist, October 2004–October 2005 (October 7, 2004), no. 29.
[430] Ibid., 1.

Holy Communion, both the past and the future are made present to us. In the Eucharist, we are united to the Lord's Last Supper, and we also receive "the pledge of eternal life," the sweetest and deepest "foretaste" of the "Heavenly banquet."[431]

With deep emotion, the pope recalls how, in 2003, the year he had dedicated to the Rosary, he issued his encyclical letter *Ecclesia de Eucharistia*. As we have seen, through this encyclical he had longed to inspire all the members of the Church to grow in their worship of and love for the Lord in the Eucharist. Now, in this apostolic letter for the Year of the Eucharist, the pope holds out to us the inspiration of the saints, whose love for the Eucharistic Lord often reduced them to tears. In a special way, we are given the example and patronage of our Blessed Mother, "woman of the Eucharist." When we receive the precious Body of the Lord in the Eucharist, we truly are receiving "the spotless flesh" of the Lord "*born of Mary*": "Ave verum corpus natum de Maria Virgine." As the pope had written in his Eucharistic encyclical, the "enraptured gaze of Mary" as she held the infant Lord Jesus gives us the "unparalleled" example of love and adoration that should fill us when we receive the Lord in the Eucharist.[432]

Inspired by our Blessed Mother and all the saints, the pope invites us to contemplate how receiving the Lord Jesus means truly "entering into a profound *communion*" with Him. The disciples on the road to Emmaus begged the Lord to *stay* with them. Even more, the Lord Himself wants *us* to stay with *Him*: "Abide in me as I abide in you" (John 15:4). This profound and mutual abiding of the Eucharistic Lord in us and of us in Him gives us a true foretaste of Heaven. Is this not everything that we most deeply

---

[431] Ibid., 3.
[432] Ibid., 1.10, 31; *Ecclesia de Eucharistia*, 6.55.

long for here on earth? The Lord has given Himself to us in the Eucharist so that we might be "*sated*" with God and taste Heaven on earth even now.[433]

This mystery of the Eucharist, which is the very "source and summit" of the Church's entire life,[434] is a mystery of the Lord's intimate *presence*, John Paul II assures us. The Eucharist is the perfect fulfilment of the Lord's promise to *remain* with us until the end of the world (Matt. 28:20).[435] When the disciples on the way to Emmaus asked Jesus to *stay with* them, He responded by giving them an infinitely greater gift than they could ever have imagined. Through the precious Sacrament of the Eucharist, He has given them, and us, the most intimate and perfect way in which He can truly stay not only *with* us but also and even more deeply *in* us, living in us so that we may live in Him.[436]

The Eucharist is the most precious fruit of the Mass, which itself is the supreme "*Sacrifice* of love" as well as the sacred *meal* that the Lord Himself prepares and hosts for us, giving us *Himself* as our feast. We must never forget that the Lord instituted the sacrament of the Eucharist on the evening of Holy Thursday, during His Last Passover meal with His beloved apostles. Giving Himself to us as our sacred meal, the pope stresses, is of the very essence of the Mass. The Lord does not *first* transform the bread and wine into His precious Body and Blood and *then* invite His apostles to partake of it—as if there were any other purpose of the Mass than our *eating* Him. No, this is the very *purpose* of the Mass, the pope assures us: the Lord Jesus wants us to *eat* His precious Body and

---

[433] St. John Paul II, *Mane Nobiscum*, 3.19.
[434] *Catechism of the Catholic Church*, 1324; *Lumen Gentium*, 11.
[435] St. John Paul II, *Mane Nobiscum*, 2.16.
[436] Ibid., 3.19.

drink His sacred Blood. "Take, *eat.* . . . This is my body." Then "He took a cup, giving it to them, and said, *drink* from it, all of you, for this is my blood" (Matt. 26:26–28).[437]

As we have seen, the Mass, the sacred meal the Lord prepares and in which He offers us *Himself* as our Feast, is also "profoundly and primarily *sacrificial.*" In the Mass, the Lord Jesus "makes present to *us*" the sacrifice of love, which He "offered once for all on Golgotha." And, as we have seen, the Mass makes present to us the past and also draws us to the future, when the Lord will come in glory at the end of time. St. John Paul II beautifully points out that this is the profoundly *Eucharistic* meaning of the Lord's sacred words: "I am *with* you always to the end of the age" (Matt. 28:20).[438]

Pope John Paul II especially urges priests and bishops, who celebrate the "great miracle of love" of the Mass, to spend time with the Lord in the Eucharist and to preside at Mass every day with the very same "joy and fervor" with which they celebrated their first Mass. The pope assures us that the Lord in the Eucharist wants to be with, and within, every one of us. Through this wonderful sacrament, we can truly know His intimate friendship, which alone satisfies our longing for love and fulfillment.[439] In the Eucharist, the Lord stays with us even to comfort us when we are sick, even to be Viaticum for us when we are dying, and to enable us to taste even now His heavenly sweetness.[440]

We also need to remember that we feed on the Lord in the Eucharist so that we may be completely transformed into Him,

[437] Ibid., 2.15.
[438] Ibid.
[439] Ibid., 30.
[440] St. John Paul II, Corpus Christi Homily, June 11, 1998, no. 5.

who came not to be served but to serve (Matt. 20:28). John Paul II again contemplates John's account of the Lord Jesus' tenderly washing His apostles' feet at the Last Supper (John 13:1–20). By humbling Himself, by bowing low before them so that He could wash their *feet*, the Lord Himself explains to us "unequivocally" the ultimate purpose and "*meaning* of the Eucharist." The Lord came to *give Himself* for us and *to* us (Mark 10:45) so that we also would give ourselves in love to one another.[441] Each one of us is here on earth for a reason and purpose that no one else can fulfill in exactly the same way. Loving the Lord and serving one another in our unique ways, let us pray and trust that others, too, will be drawn through us to the Lord as the fulfillment of their own hearts' desires.

Pope John Paul II invites us to ponder again Luke's poignant account of the two disciples traveling on the road to Emmaus. Drawn irresistibly to a seeming Stranger who walked along the way with them, they begged Him to stay with them. And they recognized their Lord and God in the "breaking of the bread." Filled with joy, the disciples then "set out immediately" to share with others the wonders they had experienced (see Luke 24:33). We, too, intimately "meet" the Lord by partaking of His precious Body and Blood in the Eucharist. The pope assures us that when we begin truly to know and love and *live* the Eucharistic Mysteries in which we are privileged to share, we ourselves will fall in love with Jesus more and more deeply and will not be able to "keep to ourselves the joy we have experienced!"[442]

May the Lord grant that this may be so for every one of us! Like the saints, may we, too, draw our very life from Jesus, who gives

---

[441] St. John Paul II, *Mane Nobiscum*, 4.28.
[442] Ibid., 4.24.

Himself so intimately to us in these Sacred Mysteries. May our own deepened love and peace draw others to discover for themselves the joy that comes from sharing in and living the glorious wonders of the Mass and the Eucharist!

Select Bibliography

Alphonsus Liguori, St. *The Holy Eucharist*. Vol. 6 of *The Complete Ascetical Works of St. Alphonsus de Liguori*. 18 vols. Edited by Eugene Grimm. New York: Benziger Brothers, 1887. Internet Archive. https://archive.org/details/alphonsusworks 06alfouoft/page/n9/mode/2up.

Ambrose of Milan, St. *On the Mysteries*. Translated by H. de Romestin, E. de Romestin, and H.T.F. Duckworth. In *Nicene and Post-Nicene Fathers*, Second Series, vol. 10, edited by Philip Schaff and Henry Wace. Buffalo, NY: Christian Literature, 1896. Revised and edited for New Advent by Kevin Knight. https://www.newadvent.org/fathers/3405.htm.

Augustine of Hippo. *Confessions*. Translated by J.G. Pilkington. In *Nicene and Post-Nicene Fathers*, First Series. Vol. 1. Edited by Philip Schaff. Buffalo, NY: Christian Literature, 1887. Revised and edited for New Advent by Kevin Knight. https://www.newadvent.org/fathers/1101.htm.

———. *Tractates on the Gospel of John*. Translated by John Gibb. In *Nicene and Post-Nicene Fathers*, First Series, vol. 7, edited by Philip Schaff. Buffalo, NY: Christian Literature, 1888. Revised and edited for New Advent by Kevin Knight. https://www.newadvent.org/fathers/1701.htm.

Bernard of Clairvaux, St. *On the Song of Songs*. E-text arranged by Darrell Wright, 2008. Internet Archive. https://archive.org/details/St.BernardOnTheSongOfSongs/mode/2up.

Catherine of Siena, St. *The Dialogue*. Translation, introduction, and notes by Suzanne Noffke, O.P. New York: Paulist Press, 1980.

———. *The Letters of St. Catherine of Siena*. Volume 1. Translated with introduction and notes by Suzanne Noffke, O.P. Binghamton, NY: Medieval and Renaissance Texts and Studies, 1988.

———. *The Letters of St. Catherine of Siena*. Volume 2. Translated with introduction and notes by Suzanne Noffke, O.P. Tempe, Arizona: Center for Medieval and Renaissance Texts and Studies, 2001.

———. *The Prayers of Catherine of Siena*. Translated and edited by Suzanne Noffke, O.P. New York: Paulist Press, 1983.

Cyril of Jerusalem, St. *Catechetical Lectures*. Translated by Edwin Hamilton Gifford. In *Nicene and Post-Nicene Fathers*, Second Series, vol. 7, edited by Philip Schaff and Henry Wace. Buffalo, NY: Christian Literature, 1894. Revised and edited for New Advent by Kevin Knight. https://www.newadvent.org/fathers/3101.htm.

Ephrem, Deacon, St. *Sermon on Our Lord*. Office of Readings for Friday of the Third Week of Easter. The Liturgy Archive. http://www.liturgies.net/Liturgies/Catholic/loh/easter/week3fridayor.htm.

Foster, Kenelm, ed. and trans. *The Life of Saint Thomas Aquinas: Biographical Documents*. Baltimore: Helicon Press, 1959.

Gregory the Great, St. *Moral Reflections on Job*. Bk. 13. Lectionary Central. http://www.lectionarycentral.com/GregoryMoralia/Book13.html.

John Chrysostom, *Baptismal Instructions*. Vol. 31 of *Ancient Christian Writers: The Works of the Fathers in Translation*. Edited by

Johannes Quasten and J. Burghardt, S.J. Translated and Annotated by Paul W. Harkins. New York: Newman Press, 1963.

——. *Homilies on First Corinthians*. Translated by Talbot W. Chambers. In *Nicene and Post-Nicene Fathers*, First Series, vol. 12, edited by Philip Schaff. Buffalo, NY: Christian Literature, 1889. Revised and edited for New Advent by Kevin Knight. http://www.newadvent.org/fathers/2201.htm.

——. *Homilies on the Acts of the Apostles*. Translated by J. Walker, J. Sheppard, and H. Browne, and revised by George B. Stevens. In *Nicene and Post-Nicene Fathers*, First Series, vol. 11, edited by Philip Schaff. Buffalo, NY: Christian Literature, 1889. Revised and edited for New Advent by Kevin Knight. http://www.newadvent.org/fathers/2101.htm.

——. *Homilies on First Thessalonians*. Translated by John A. Broadus. In *Nicene and Post-Nicene Fathers*, First Series, vol. 13, edited by Philip Schaff. Buffalo, NY: Christian Literature, 1889. Revised and edited for New Advent by Kevin Knight. https://www.newadvent.org/fathers/2304.htm.

——. *Homilies on the Gospel of John*. Translated by Charles Marriott. In Nicene and Post-Nicene Fathers, First Series, vol. 14, edited by Philip Schaff. Buffalo, NY: Christian Literature, 1889. Revised and edited for New Advent by Kevin Knight. https://www.newadvent.org/fathers/2401.htm.

——. *On the Priesthood*. Bk. 3. Translated by W. R. W. Stephens. In *Nicene and Post-Nicene Fathers*, First Series, vol. 9, edited by Philip Schaff. Buffalo, NY: Christian Literature, 1889. Revised and edited for New Advent by Kevin Knight. https://www.newadvent.org/fathers/19223.htm.

John Damascene, St. *An Exposition of the Orthodox Faith*. Translated by E. W. Watson and L. Pullan. In *Nicene and Post-Nicene Fathers*, Second Series, vol. 9, edited by Philip Schaff and Henry Wace.

Buffalo, NY: Christian Literature, 1899. Revised and edited for New Advent by Kevin Knight. https://www.newadvent.org/fathers/33044.htm.

John Paul II, Pope St. Encyclical letter *Ecclesia de Eucharistia* (April 17, 2003).

———. Apostolic letter *Mane Nobiscum Domine* for the Year of the Eucharist, October 2004–October 2005 (October 7, 2004).

Leo the Great, Pope St., *Letter 31 to Pulcheria*. Translated by Charles Lett Feltoe. In *Nicene and Post-Nicene Fathers*, Second Series, vol. 12, edited by Philip Schaff and Henry Wace. Buffalo, NY: Christian Literature, 1895. Revised and edited for New Advent by Kevin Knight. https://www.newadvent.org/fathers/3604031.htm.

———. *Sermons of St. Leo the Great*. Translated by Charles Lett Feltoe. In *Nicene and Post-Nicene Fathers*, Second Series, vol. 12, edited by Philip Schaff and Henry Wace. Buffalo, NY: Christian Literature, 1895. Revised and edited for New Advent by Kevin Knight. http://www.newadvent.org/fathers/3603.htm.

———. *Sermon 66: Fifteenth Sermon on the Lord's Passion*. Office of Readings for Thursday of the Fourth Week of Lent. Liturgy Archive. https://www.liturgies.net/Liturgies/Catholic/loh/lent/week4thursdayor.htm.

Newman, John Henry, St. *Apologia pro Vita Sua*. (1865). London: Longmans, Green, 1908. National Institute for Newman Studies. https://www.newmanreader.org/works/apologia65/index.html.

———. *The Church of the Fathers: St. Chrysostom, Theodoret, Mission of St. Benedict, Benedictine Schools*. Vol. 2 of *Historical Sketches*. London: Longmans, Green, 1906. National Institute for Newman Studies. https://www.newmanreader.org/works/historical/volume2/index.html.

——. *Discourses to Mixed Congregations.* London: Longmans, Green, 1906. National Institute for Newman Studies. https://www.newmanreader.org/works/discourses/index.html#titlepage.

——. *Discussions and Arguments on Various Subjects.* London: Longmans, Green, 1907. National Institute for Newman Studies. https://www.newmanreader.org/works/arguments/index.html#titlepage.

——. *Faith and Prejudice and Other Sermons.* Edited by the Birmingham Oratory. New York: Sheed and Ward, 1956. National Institute for Newman Studies. https://www.newmanreader.org/works/ninesermons/index.html.

——. *Meditations and Devotions.* Edited by Rev. W. P. Neville. London: Longmans, Green, 1907. National Institute for Newman Studies. https://newmanreader.org/works/meditations/.

——. *Parochial and Plain Sermons.* Vol. 3. London: Longmans, Green, 1907. National Institute for Newman Studies. https://newmanreader.org/works/parochial/volume3/index.html.

——. *Parochial and Plain Sermons.* Vol. 4. London: Longmans, Green, 1907. National Institute for Newman Studies. https://www.newmanreader.org/works/parochial/volume4/index.html.

——. *Parochial and Plain Sermons.* Vol. 6. London: Longmans, Green, 1907. National Institute for Newman Studies. https://www.newmanreader.org/works/parochial/volume6/index.html.

——. *Parochial and Plain Sermons.* Vol. 7. London: Longmans, Green, 1907. National Institute for Newman Studies. https://www.newmanreader.org/works/parochial/volume7/index.html.

——. *Sermons Bearing on Subjects of the Day.* London: Longmans, Green, 1902. National Institute for Newman Studies. https://newmanreader.org/works/subjects/index.html.

——. *Sermon Notes of John Henry Cardinal Newman 1849–1878.* Edited by the Fathers of the Birmingham Oratory. London:

Longmans, Green, 1913. National Institute for Newman Studies. https://www.newmanreader.org/works/sermonnotes/index.html.

———. *Sermons Preached on Various Occasions*. London: Longmans, Green, 1908. National Institute for Newman Studies. https://www.newmanreader.org/works/occasions/index.html.

Raymond of Capua. *The Life of Catherine of Siena*. Translated with introduction and notes by Conleth Kearns, O.P. Wilmington, DE: Michael Glazier, 1980.

Seton, Elizabeth Bayley, St., *Collected Writings*. Vol. 1, *Correspondence and Journals 1793–1808*. Edited by Regina Bechtle, S.C., and Judith Metz, S.C. New York: New City Press, 2000. Vincentian Digital Books, 9. https://via.library.depaul.edu/vincentian_ebooks/9.

———. *Collected Writings*. Vol. 2, Correspondence and Journals 1808–1820. Edited by Regina Bechtle, S.C., and Judith Metz, S.C. New York: New City Press, 2002. Vincentian Digital Books, https://via.library.depaul.edu/vincentian_ebooks/11.

Teresa of Avila, St. *The Way of Perfection*. Translated and edited by E. Allison Peers. New York: Image Books, 1964. Scanned by Harry Plantinga, 1995. Online Christian Library. https://onlinechristianlibrary.com/author/st-teresa-of-avila/.

Thérèse of Lisieux, St. *Letters of St. Thérèse of Lisieux*. Vol. 1, *1877–1890*. Translated by John Clarke, O.C.D. Washington, D.C.: ICS Publications, 1982.

———. *Letters of St. Thérèse of Lisieux*. Vol. 2, *1890–1897*. Translated by John Clarke, O.C.D. Washington, D.C.: ICS Publications, 1982.

———. *Story of a Soul*. Translated by John Clarke, O.C.D. Washington, D.C.: ICS Publications, 1976.

———. *St. Thérèse of Lisieux General Correspondence.* Vol. 1. Translated by John Clarke, O.C.D. Washington, D.C., Institute of Carmelite Studies, 1982.

Thérèse of Lisieux: Her Last Conversations. Translated by John Clarke, O.C.D. Washington, D.C.: ICS Publications, 1977.

Thomas Aquinas, St. *Commentary on the Gospel of St. John.* Part I: Chapters 1–7. Translated by James A. Weisheipl, O.P. Albany: Magi Books, 1980. Calibre Library. https://isidore.co/aquinas/John6.htm.

———. *Commentary on the Gospel of St. John.* Part II: Chapters 8–21. Translated by Fabian R. Larcher, O.P. Albany: Magi Books, 1998. St. Isidore E-book Library. https://isidore.co/aquinas/english/SSJohn.htm.

———. *Commentary on the First Epistle to the Corinthians.* Translated by Fabian Larcher, O.P. (987-1046 by Daniel Keating). Html-edited by Joseph Kenny, O.P. St. Isidore E-book Library. https://isidore.co/aquinas/english/SS1Cor.htm#114.

———. *Expositio in Symbolum Apostolorum, The Apostles' Creed.* Translated by Joseph B. Collins. New York, 1939. Edited and html-formatted by Joseph Kenny, O.P. St. Isidore E-book Library. https://isidore.co/aquinas/Creed.htm#4.

———. *Summa Theologiae.* 2nd and rev. ed. 1920. Translated by Fathers of the English Dominican Province. New Advent. http://home.newadvent.org/summa/.

Vianney, John Baptist Mary, St. *The Eucharistic Meditations of the Curé d'Ars.* Carmelite Publications, 1961. India Document. https://vdocument.in/the-eucharistic-meditations-of-st-john-vianney.html.

———. *Catechetical Instructions.* Crossroads Initiative. https://www.crossroadsinitiative.com/media/articles/catechetical-instructions/.

The Wonders of the Mass and the Eucharist

Witnesses of the Apostolic Canonization Process of Thérèse of Lisieux,
  1915–1916. Archives du Carmel de Lisieux. https://archives.
  carmeldelisieux.fr/en/.

Witnesses of the Ordinary Canonization Process of Thérèse of Lisieux,
  1910–1911. Archives du Carmel de Lisieux. https://archives.
  carmeldelisieux.fr/en/.

Index of Scriptural Citations

The Wonders of the Mass and the Eucharist

Index of Names and Subjects

The Wonders of the Mass and the Eucharist

bread and wine, 19, 20, 21,
22, 176; of contemplative
prayer, 6, 63; the Lord's gift
of Himself in the Eucharist,
13, 23, 24, 35, 36, 91, 104,
107, 108, 114, 119, 120,
121, 122, 124, 136, 142,
146, 159, 172, 173, 174,
182; of faith, 30; of sanctifying grace, 23, 56
gladness, 116
glory, of heaven, 69, 177; of
Jesus, 40, 70, 89, 106, 124,
125, 183; of risen body, 69
God. See Trinity; Father; Jesus;
Holy Spirit
Golgotha, 183
Good Friday, 129, 138
Gorbachev, Mikhail, 170
grace, sanctifying, 13, 14, 17,
23, 53, 55, 56, 57, 60, 61,
69, 74, 77, 78, 88, 136, 151
graciousness, 49, 74, 113
gratitude, 4, 9, 12, 42, 79, 96,
107, 109, 121, 133, 146,
151, 153, 164, 172, 174
Gregory the Great, Pope, St., 16
Gregory X, Pope, 50
grief, 97, 100
Guérin family, 128
Guérin, Marie, 128, 144

hands, 20, 24, 40, 66, 105, 138,
150
happiness, 57, 104, 112, 132,
137, 151

healing, 39, 56, 60, 61, 73, 77,
88, 91, 125, 145, 158, 160,
161, 165
heart, 6, 10, 20, 25, 29, 30, 49,
58, 66, 73, 79, 82, 89, 100,
101, 108, 110, 126, 144, 166,
172, 184; of Jesus, 23, 33,
62, 63, 64, 65, 80, 81, 85, 90,
145, 153, 159, 161, 163, 179
heartaches, 7
Heaven, 29, 36, 41, 67, 68, 76,
80, 83, 85, 114, 132, 173;
Communion of Saints in
Heaven, 178; Divine Liturgy
of the Mass and Heaven, 15,
20-21, 25, 40-41, 97, 118,
126, 131, 142, 143, 151;
the Father's Heaven within
us, 23; Heaven within us
through the Eucharist, 24,
62, 63, 64, 65, 69, 70, 89,
97, 104, 107, 109, 118, 119,
121, 126, 131, 132, 136,
148, 149, 151, 153, 165,
177, 181, 182, 183; Heaven
within the tabernacle, 152;
154; the Trinity's Heaven
within us, 57, 136
Hebrews, 37
help, of the angels, 117; our
Blessed Mother's help, 100;
the Lord's help, 3, 81, 91,
150, 153, 159, 160, 162; for
one another, 43, 44, 48, 74,
77, 107, 113, 156, 157, 168;

The Wonders of the Mass and the Eucharist

The Wonders of the Mass and the Eucharist

"Pange Lingua," 66, 68
"Panis Angelicus," 47, 63, 66
pardon, 153
parents, 37, 108, 138, 155
Paris, 48, 134, 144
Parkinson's disease, 167, 170
Paschal Lamb, 37, 85, 151
Passion, of the Lord Jesus, 31,
    51, 52, 69, 156, 162, 173
Passover Meal, 32, 182
Paul, St., Apostle, 17, 20, 29,
    34, 41, 42, 43, 99, 116
Paul VI, Pope St., 95, 168, 169
peace, 6, 7, 17, 33, 39, 41, 44,
    63, 64, 74, 78, 80, 82, 85,
    95, 107, 112, 144, 151, 153,
    162, 178, 185
pelican, 68, 76
Penance, Sacrament of, 61, 77,
    78, 81, 106, 133, 147, 156
Pentecost, 10, 11, 117, 163
Peter, St., 20, 77, 120, 154
Philip Neri, St., 112
Pius X, Pope St., 127, 130, 145,
    146
Pius XI, Pope, 130, 146
Pius XII, Pope Venerable, 168
poor, 40, 49, 66, 146; care
    for, 28, 43-44, 72, 73, 112,
    147, 156
poverty, 48, 86, 107, 147
praise, 11, 19, 20, 21, 25, 66, 67,
    68, 78, 151, 172, 173, 178
prayer, 6, 15, 47, 48, 49, 68, 70,
    84, 88, 98, 116, 126, 148,

165; before the Blessed Sac-
    rament, 102, 133, 159-163,
    159-163; Church at prayer,
    115-117; contemplative, 6,
    63, 153; after Holy Com-
    munion, 87-91, 163-166;
    intercessory prayer, 22, 45,
    75, 77, 126, 127, 143, 166;
    for the dead, 22; of the
    Mass, 19, 20, 22, 23; the
    Lord's Prayer, 22, 23, 87
priests, 9, 11, 12, 20, 21, 34,
    40, 54, 78, 84, 99, 112, 114,
    122, 123, 137, 147, 148,
    155, 160, 173, 176, 183
problems, 3, 62, 87, 107, 164,
    172
processions, Eucharistic, 68,
    100, 113, 131, 171-173
publican, 136

Raymond of Capua, 72n177,
    73, 74, 76, 79, 80
Reconciliation, Sacrament of,
    61, 77, 78, 81, 106, 133,
    147, 156
redemption, 16, 50, 68, 70, 156
Redemptorists, 156, 157
Reginald of Piperno, 48, 49
repentance, 42, 60, 61, 83
resurrection, of human beings,
    69, 151, 177; of Jesus, 4, 9,
    10, 11, 12, 14, 15, 16, 18,
    19, 21, 27, 31, 52, 53, 162,
    175, 180
revelation, mysteries of, 123

Rome, 11, 16, 49, 74, 75, 111,
112, 128, 134, 167, 169,
170, 171
Rosary, 181

sacrament, 4, 12, 13, 14, 15, 16,
52, 53, 54, 62, 139, 177, 179
Sacrifice, of the Mass, 11, 13,
21, 22, 35, 40, 42, 53, 108,
114, 115, 121, 126, 166,
175, 176, 182, 183
sacrilege, 144, 145
"Sacris Solemniis," 66
sadness, 6, 81, 132, 133
saints, 4, 6, 7, 26, 29, 45, 64,
67, 103, 126, 138, 158, 159,
169, 173, 175, 178, 179,
181, 184
sanctifying grace, see grace
Scripture, 19, 28, 51, 111, 120,
137
scrupulosity, 144, 157
seminarians, 109
Seton, Anna Maria, 94, 96, 97,
101, 102
Seton, Cecilia, 107, 109n262
Seton, Elizabeth Ann Bayley,
St., 93-110
Seton, Rebecca, 95, 96, 97n235,
98, 99, 100, 101, 102
Seton, William, 93-94, 96-97
sickness, 22, 71, 73, 91, 99,
116, 139, 150, 161, 183
side of the Lord, pierced, 38,
39, 52, 72, 75, 77, 79, 80,
81, 82

Sign of the Cross, 100
sins, 15, 19, 22, 42, 51, 52, 78,
81, 83, 84, 136, 144, 145,
176; mortal, 61; venial, 56,
60-61
singing, 14, 15n10, 24, 67, 68
Sisters of Charity of St.
Joseph's, 95
sleeplessness, 139, 157
Son, God the; see Jesus
song, 165
soul, 6, 14, 23, 25, 37, 43, 51,
69, 71, 74, 88, 91, 103, 108,
114, 132, 136, 149, 151,
152, 163, 165, 166; Heaven
of Jesus, 136, 166; Heaven
of the Trinity, 136
sorrow, 19, 33, 36, 61, 66, 78,
95, 96, 97, 99, 100, 102,
132, 153
species of bread and wine, 37,
54, 71, 89, 124, 136
spirits, evil. See demons.
spiritual Communion, 55-56,
73, 156, 165, 166
St. John, Ambrose, 113
Stations of the Cross of St.
Alphonsus Liguori, 156
Story of a Soul, 129, 141, 142
struggles, 39, 62, 103, 139,
147, 157
study, 48, 49, 94, 110, 111,
112, 167
suffering, 22, 50, 72, 73, 88, 96,
97, 100, 113, 129, 135, 138,

About the Author

Sr. Mary Ann Fatula, O.P., Ph.D., served as a professor of theology at Ohio Dominican University and for more than thirty years taught theology there. Sr. Mary Ann is the author of *Catherine of Siena's Way*, *The Holy Spirit: Unbounded Gift of Joy*, *Thomas Aquinas: Preacher and Friend*, *Heaven's Splendor*, and *Drawing Close to the Holy Spirit*.

Sophia Institute

Sophia Institute is a nonprofit institution that seeks to nurture the spiritual, moral, and cultural life of souls and to spread the gospel of Christ in conformity with the authentic teachings of the Roman Catholic Church.

Sophia Institute Press fulfills this mission by offering translations, reprints, and new publications that afford readers a rich source of the enduring wisdom of mankind.

Sophia Institute also operates the popular online resource CatholicExchange.com. *Catholic Exchange* provides world news from a Catholic perspective as well as daily devotionals and articles that will help readers to grow in holiness and live a life consistent with the teachings of the Church.

In 2013, Sophia Institute launched Sophia Institute for Teachers to renew and rebuild Catholic culture through service to Catholic education. With the goal of nurturing the spiritual, moral, and cultural life of souls, and an abiding respect for the role and work of teachers, we strive to provide materials and programs that are at once enlightening to the mind and ennobling to the heart; faithful and complete, as well as useful and practical.

Sophia Institute gratefully recognizes the Solidarity Association for preserving and encouraging the growth of our apostolate over the course of many years. Without their generous and timely support, this book would not be in your hands.

www.SophiaInstitute.com
www.CatholicExchange.com
www.SophiaInstituteforTeachers.org

Sophia Institute Press is a registered trademark of Sophia Institute.
Sophia Institute is a tax-exempt institution as defined by the
Internal Revenue Code, Section 501(c)(3). Tax ID 22-2548708.